AN EVALUATION PRIMER

by Arlene Fink and Jacqueline Kosecoff

Forewords by Charles E. Lewis and Wilson Riles

© 1978 by Capitol Publications, Inc.

For information contact Capitol Publications, Inc., 2430 Pennsylvania Avenue N.W., Washington, DC 20037. Telephone 202/452-1600.

ISBN 0-917870-02-6 (cloth)
ISBN 0-917870-06-9 (paper)
Library of Congress Catalog Card Number 77-088461

Library of Congress Cataloging in Publication Data

Fink, Arlene.
    An evaluation primer.

    Bibliography: p.
    Includes index.
    1. Evaluation research (Social action programs)
I. Kosecoff, Jacqueline B., joint author.   II. Title.
H62.F435   300'.1'8   77-88461
ISBN 0-917870-02-6

TABLE
OF
CONTENTS

About the authors

Arlene Fink and Jacqueline Kosecoff direct the Los Angeles office of Steiger, Fink & Kosecoff, Inc., a research and development firm with broad experience in conducting evaluations and training evaluators for education and health programs.

Dr. Arlene Fink is on the Faculty of the School of Medicine at the University of California, Los Angeles, where she is an advisor to the Robert Wood Johnson Foundation's Clinical Scholars Program and a member of the senior research staff of the Health Services Research Center. She has directed many evaluations, including studies for the Experimental Medical Care Review Organizations and the California Preschool Program, and has testified before the California legislature as an evaluation specialist. Dr. Fink has also developed a series of workshops to introduce educators and health professionals to evaluation theory and techniques. She was educated at City College of New York and Columbia University, and received her doctorate from UCLA.

Dr. Jacqueline Kosecoff has directed major evaluation studies for the National Institutes of Health and the National Endowment for the Humanities. While on the faculty of the Center for the Study of Evaluation, she was director of the research group on criterion-referenced measurement and criterion-referenced testing and the evaluation services and training unit. Dr. Kosecoff is a member of the faculty of the UCLA School of Medicine where she teaches courses in evaluation and research methodology. She received her Master's Degree in applied mathematics from Brown University and was one of the first in the country to receive a doctorate in evaluation and research (from UCLA).

Together, the authors have conducted evaluations for the National Center for Health Services Research, the National Institute of Education, the University of Southern California Medical Center, the National Science Foundation, the UCLA School of Medicine, the Office of Education, the RAND Corporation, and American Institute for Research.

FOREWORD I

"Everybody's doing it, doing it, doing it . . ." The title of an old song presently is very applicable to the topic of this book. Beginning in the late 1960s, an increased emphasis on "evaluation" has turned into an almost obsessional preoccupation. The only problem is not everybody is doing it well. In fact, the majority of evaluative activities, either to facilitate program management or to examine the impact of an effort, are rather ill conceived and/or poorly conducted. This personal opinion of the quality of evaluative research is based upon considerable experience in reviewing research proposals for federal agencies and foundations, as well as manuscripts submitted to journals reflecting the performance of "evaluation."

Certainly there is no shortage of encouragement from agencies for these pursuits, nor are there deficits in the card catalogs of libraries under the heading "evaluation." Many books have been published over the past few years on the evaluation of social action programs. The majority of these, however, are written in highly technical language and many are most appropriate for graduate students, or those already familiar with the problems of the field and already engaged in the conduct of evaluative studies. This volume is exactly what its title says, "a primer." It is written in a way that helps to de-mystify the business of evaluation for all those who are concerned with it, but do not have a particular past history.

The authors set forth in sequential chapters the various stages that must be pursued in such efforts, and include "do it yourself" exercises at the end of these sections, so that the reader may conduct a self-evaluation as to the achievement of the objectives of the chapter.

For those in the health field, I believe chapter two on the formulation of evaluation questions may be the most critical. Too often in the health field, the specific objectives of an effort are poorly defined, either by those responsible for the implementation of the program, or those paying the bill. As this book points out, one can hardly evaluate that which one cannot define. It would behoove all of us, regardless of past experience, to periodically run through the checklist provided in this and subsequent chapters. It is easy, under the pressure of time and other commitments, to omit or bypass certain activities. Perhaps this volume might be thought of as an equivalent to the checklist performed by a pilot at the end of the runway. A quick review of objectives, instruments, etc., before takeoff is an effective way of avoiding pilot errors, major/minor disasters, or acquiring fear of evaluating.

Charles E. Lewis, M.D., Sc.D.
Professor of Medicine
University of California, Los Angeles

FOREWORD II

If I were to define evaluation in simple terms, I would say it is a process through which we attempt to answer some basic questions about what we hoped to do and then what we actually accomplished. In addition, through the evaluation process we compare our accomplishments with our objectives and ask ourselves, "What changes do we have to make to come closer to our objectives?" If, on the other hand, I were asked to define the evaluation process in more technical language, I would probably outline it in this way:

1. Define the objectives.
2. Using evaluation measures and techniques, determine the outcome of efforts to reach the stated objectives.
3. Interpret the findings from the data gathered.
4. Develop procedures for implementing necessary changes.

In examining Arlene Fink's and Jacqueline Kosecoff's book on evaluation, it seems to me that they have, as the title of their book suggests, given us an elementary lesson in the evaluation process without resorting to the highly technical language of the professional evaluator. At the same time, however, they have introduced some basic language in evaluation that educators should have in their vocabulary. Yet, the authors' focus is on the process, not the language. And, as you will note by reading the document, authors Fink and Kosecoff have included considerably more steps in the evaluation process than I included in my simple definition, and their detailed approach should be particularly helpful to those who have not had instruction in evaluation procedures.

I am very conscious of the importance of evaluation to education. The people of California spend approximately $6.5 billion per year for the education of over five million children and adults, and they want to know what they are getting for their money. One significant question, which has been asked from the very beginning of public education, is still being asked: "Are the schools teaching our children to read, write, and compute?" But in today's society the people are asking other more difficult questions: "Are current instructional methods working?" "Are there better methods?" "What will happen if we invest more funds in education?" "Where and how can improvement best be made?" The answers to these questions and a great many more can be provided by those who understand and use the evaluation process effectively. Thus, it is critical that today's educators not only know testing procedures but also know the total evaluation process. This new book can give educators and others a good introduction to the procedures for evaluating the worth, quality, significance, and condition of educational programs. Of course, the authors have not restricted themselves to evaluation in education. They have dealt with evaluation in all social action programs—those programs that provide health, education, and welfare services.

I believe the authors would agree that a well-designed evaluation program can serve many purposes. It can provide a basis for determining a child's growth in a particular subject area and for grouping children for learning purposes. It can be used for reporting accomplishments, problems and financial data to parents and taxpayers. But a good evaluation program can also do more. It can provide a framework for guiding each child or adult in the learning process and for establishing the very important working relationships we must have with the parents and the community for promoting effective educational activities. And, finally, a sound evaluation process is essential for analyzing and improving the basic philosophy and structure of the public schools. Therefore, I am pleased that Arlene Fink and Jacqueline Kosecoff have given us a book that spells out the evaluation process in simple terms.

Wilson Riles
Superintendent of Public Instruction
State of California

PREFACE

The purpose of this book is to enable you to conduct and interpret evaluations of social programs. During the past decade, evaluation theory and methodology has grown by a dual process of invention and adhesion, and the demand for people with the diverse range of skills required of an evaluator has increased very rapidly. Although there are monographs about evaluation theories and models and texts about psychometrics and statistics, no books are available that synthesize in a usable way the procedures for conducting an evaluation. The hapless reader is thus forced first to combine knowledge from a variety of disciplines and then to translate the results into strategies for performing evaluation tasks. One of our reasons for writing this book was to meet the demand among students, scientists, evaluators and administrators of social and health programs for an evaluation primer. However, this was not our only motive. As instructors in courses about evaluation, we found we had to make up for the lack of a standard textbook by creating one each time we taught. Our students include physicians, pharmacists, nurses, public health personnel, professional educators, school administrators, teachers, social scientists, and evaluation specialists. Each of them has differing evaluation needs. Since we couldn't find a book in which we had confidence, we decided to write one ourselves.

When planning *An Evaluation Primer,* we recalled that Roger Bacon said that knowledge is acquired in two ways, by reasoning and by experience. In this book we have tried to fuse our knowledge about evaluation methods with our day-to-day experience in working with clients and providing information to policy makers. Each chapter explains in detail how to perform evaluation activities and also gives a number of examples drawn from actual experience. In addition, two workbooks—one focusing on education and one on health—provide opportunities to practice evaluation activities. The workbooks contain a series of exercises with answers that are keyed to each chapter.

An Evaluation Primer has as its premise that an evaluation must provide the people who commission it with information that is technically sound, useful, and believable. Although many other people might use evaluation information, the evaluator cannot be accountable to everyone. We also take the position that the evaluator's main task is to provide information and not to make decisons about how to use it. Consequently, although the evaluator is encouraged to take an active role in framing evaluation studies, we believe it is the responsibility of the sponsors and of the people who will use the findings to define the evaluation questions and criteria.

We have deliberately chosen to focus *An Evaluation Primer* on the basic procedures involved in evaluating existing social action programs and have not discussed several other issues of importance to evaluation specialists. These include evaluation theories and the politics and ethics of evaluation. We hope to discuss topics such as cost benefit analysis and needs assessment strategies in future books.

Finally, we want to thank some of the people who worked with us. The preparation of *An Evaluation Primer* would not have been possible without the help of Emily Harris, whose editorial contributions salvaged much of our prose and made it readable. Dr. Charles E.Lewis and Dr. Wilson Riles, who graciously wrote introductions to the book, deserve very special thanks.

Neither of us could have written this book alone. Lewis Carroll, in *Through the Looking-Glass,* sums up in a bit of whimsy our feelings of mutual dependence and gratitude.

> "Seven years and six months!" Humpty Dumpty repeated thoughtfully. "An uncomfortable sort of age. Now if you'd asked *my* advice, I'd have said, 'Leave off at seven'—but it's too late now."
>
> "I never ask advice about growing," Alice said indignantly .... "I mean," she said, "that one can't help growing older."
>
> "*One* can't perhaps," said Humpty Dumpty, "but *two* can. With proper assistance you might have left off at seven."

Each of us constantly provided the other with proper assistance.

Arlene Fink
Jacqueline Kosecoff

Los Angeles, 1977

AN EVALUATION PRIMER

by Arlene Fink and Jacqueline Kosecoff

Forewords by Charles E. Lewis and Wilson Riles

CHAPTER 1
AN INTRODUCTION TO EVALUATION

Evaluation is a set of procedures to appraise a program's merit and to provide information about its goals, activities, outcomes, impact and costs.

Almost any program or product can be evaluated. For example, it is possible to evaluate a reading textbook, a bilingual mathematics program, an anti-smoking program, a new antihistamine drug, or a quality care audit system. While it is possible to assess the merit of virtually any program or product, it may not always be useful to do so. Evaluations are typically conducted only when the purposes and characteristics of the program or product are known and when it is anticipated that if the program or product is good enough, it will be used again.

Anyone who needs information regarding a program's merit is a potential user of evaluation findings. For example, the authors of a venereal disease education program could use information from an evaluation of their program to justify revising its objectives or modifying its instructional strategies. Educators might use information from an evaluation of who benefits from the program to decide whether or not to adopt it in their community. Finally, the agency that funded the program could use the evaluation information to decide whether or not to refund it.

WHY EVALUATE?

There are two kinds of evaluations. One is to improve a program and the other is to determine the effectiveness of a program. Improvement and effectiveness evaluations are always distinguished from one another by how information is used rather than by the kinds of information collected or the stage at which it is gathered. In an improvement context, evaluation information is used to modify and improve a program; in an effectiveness context, information is used to establish the program's quality and outcomes.

The Improvement Evaluation

The purpose of an improvement evaluation is to determine how a program can be upgraded and refined. Improvement information is typically requested by the creators and organizers of a still-developing program. These people may ask questions like:

Were staff available at the designated hours?

Were the participants in the program the ones for whom it was intended?

Answers to questions like these help to explain the causes of a program's strengths and weaknesses and indicate where modifications might need to be made.

Other questions frequently asked in an improvement evaluation concern how much progress a program is making toward accomplishing its objectives. Typical questions requiring progress information are:

By the end of the unit can students read the words "dog" and "cat"?

During the first semester, did students benefit from classroom discussions?

Evaluations conducted for improvement focus on finding out what goes on within a program. Because of this, comparisons with other programs are not as useful as information about how well the program itself has been implemented and how well it is achieving its goals.

The Effectiveness Evaluation

The purpose of an effectiveness evaluation is to appraise a program's overall impact and to determine the consistency with which it produces certain outcomes. Effectiveness evaluations are usually requested by a program's sponsors, its potential participants, and by legislators. Several types of evaluation information are frequently collected in an effectiveness context. One type involves identifying how well a program's goals have been met. This means asking questions like:

Did the Family Practice Clinic succeed in (meeting its goal of) involving the entire family in each individual member's health care?

Did our state's compensatory education program (meet its goal to) encourage parents to take active roles in making decisions about their children's education?

Another type of effectiveness evaluation information involves determining the impact of a program for special groups. An example of an evaluation question that requires this information is:

Are there differences among Black, Anglo, and Spanish-heritage students with respect to their attitudes toward the health education program?

Still other types of information needed for an effectiveness evaluation focus on the comparative value of a program and examine its side effects and costs. This information is required to answer questions like:

Is the ARTC or the ORT treatment program more successful in managing hypertension?

What are the costs of the new program in terms of its finances, facilities and staff?

In summary, evaluations to determine effectiveness provide information about all potential program participants and all comparable programs.

WHAT ACTIVITIES ARE INVOLVED IN CONDUCTING EVALUATIONS?

Evaluators may be asked to supervise or conduct a number of activities, and it is helpful to organize them into seven major categories:
1. Formulating credible evaluation questions ✓
2. Constructing evaluation designs
3. Planning information collection
4. Collecting evaluation information
5. Planning and conducting information analyses

6. Reporting evaluation information
7. Managing an evaluation

When selecting an evaluator for small evaluation projects, it is probably best to choose someone with a wide variety of skills and experience. For larger evaluations, an evaluation team might include people with highly specialized skills in statistics or report writing.

Formulating Credible Questions

To be effective, an evaluation must produce timely and believable information that is useful in improving or establishing the effectiveness of a program. To guarantee an evaluation's quality, the evaluator must formulate questions that will give clients the information they need. To do this, the evaluator must first get to know the program's goals and activities and the kinds of information that will be acceptable as evidence of program merit.

In an improvement evaluation the evaluator works closely with program staff and participants, and evaluation questions are usually about whether the program has been implemented as planned and whether it is making progress toward achieving its goals. In an effectiveness evaluation, the evaluator usually works for a program's sponsors or other agencies interested in accrediting and adopting the program. Their evaluation questions are generally about the program's overall success in meeting its goals, its applicability to special situations or with special groups, its comparative value, and whether there are any special consequences of participation in the program.

Constructing Evaluation Designs

Constructing an evaluation design involves deciding how people will be grouped and which variables will be manipulated during an evaluation. As part of the process, the evaluator must identify independent and dependent variables and assess the internal and external validity of the design.

Improvement evaluations often use case studies and other noncomparison design strategies, while effectiveness evaluations tend to use more powerful designs that involve comparison groups.

Planning Information Collection

To plan information collection activities it is necessary to consider the evaluation questions, the information collection techniques, and the design strategy that is used to group and sample subjects and to structure the information analysis.

In an improvement evaluation, the evaluator can sometimes use new techniques and instruments that have not been exhaustively validated, and the program staff may actively assist in information collection. In an effectiveness evaluation, however, the evaluator must always use validated techniques and instruments and should rely on individuals who are not affiliated with the program for information collection.

Collecting Evaluation Information

Information collection activities require the evaluator to hire and train information collectors, to pilot test and obtain clearance for the information collection procedures and instruments, and finally, to collect the evaluation information.

Once again, the nature of information collection activities will be influenced by the purpose of the evaluation. The evaluator may find it necessary to create and validate new collection instruments for an improvement evaluation since existing measures may not fit the emerging program. For an effectiveness evaluation, however, the evaluator should use instruments that have been validated and are known to provide information at the desired levels of precision.

Planning and Conducting Information Analyses

The analysis of evaluation information is the process of summarizing and synthesizing the data to find the answers to the evaluation questions. Information analysis involves preparing the evaluation data for analysis, applying the appropriate analytic methods, and interpreting the results.

In an improvement evaluation, the evaluator usually can be flexible and creative in applying analysis methods to get the most information about the success of the program and its constitutent parts. In an effectiveness evaluation, on the other hand, the evaluator should select well-defined analytic methods that will permit inferences regarding the program's value in comparison to other programs and the broad consequences of participation in it.

Reporting Evaluation Information

The evaluator is responsible for reporting evaluation information to clients when it is needed and in a form that is easy to use. In an improvement evaluation, the evaluator usually provides frequent reports to the program staff. These may include formal written reports, memorandums, presentations at meetings, or telephone calls. For an effectiveness evaluation, the evaluator usually prepares a few formal and very detailed reports.

Managing an Evaluation

Management of an evaluation involves preparing and following a schedule of activities; assigning evaluation staff and consultants to specific evaluation tasks; and developing and adhering to budgets.

WHAT ARE INTERNAL AND EXTERNAL EVALUATORS?

Regular staff members who take responsibility for evaluation activities are called internal evaluators, while outside consultants are called external evaluators. Internal evaluators have the advantage of being closer to the program and its staff and consequently less obtrusive. They are less likely to be objective than an outside evaluator, however, because they are personally involved in the program and because their job depends upon it. External evaluators, on the other hand, have the advantage of being objective and of having a fresh perspective. Their disadvantages are their image as outsider-critics and sometimes their physical isolation from the program.

In improvement evaluations, it is possible to use either an internal or external evaluator since the evaluation is likely to require close contact with the project and staff. Even an external evaluator can be expected to become somewhat involved in a project that grows because of his or her recommendations. In effectiveness evaluations, however, the evaluator should be an outsider who is professionally independent of the effect of any recommendations or the good will of the program staff.

It is generally better to use an external evaluator than an internal evaluator, regardless of the evaluation's context. External evaluators are more likely to be objective and to have an independent perspective, and as a result, the evaluation's findings are more likely to be accepted.

CHAPTER 2
FORMULATING CREDIBLE EVALUATION QUESTIONS

To be effective, an evaluation must be believable and useful to those who must apply its findings to improve the program or certify its worth. To ensure credibility, an evaluator must:

1. *Understand completely the program's goals and activities.* To get to know a program's goals and activities, the evaluator should become familiar with the political and historical circumstances that created the program; its physical location (e.g., a clinic or school); its organizational structure; its staff; and any documents, reports, or products produced by the program (e.g., a proposal, an annual report, a film, a review procedure).

2. *Find out what kind of information will be accepted as convincing evidence of the program's merit.* There are many different ways to prove that a program is worthwhile. The evaluator must decide what information will provide the most believable evidence of the program's merit to the individuals who must use the evaluation's findings.

3. *Formulate specific questions that the evaluation's clients want answered.* The evaluator must know what kind of information the client needs. To do this, evaluations should be designed to answer the client's questions and to provide information about program merit.

4. *Make sure the client understands the procedures and products of the evaluation.* The evaluator must make sure that the client understands what an evaluation is, the reasons for conducting the evaluation, and the way evaluation information will be presented.

To ensure proper attention to these four considerations, two special documents should be used. These documents are the Evaluator's Program Description (EPD) and the Evaluation Questions (EQ).

THE EVALUATOR'S PROGRAM DESCRIPTION (EPD)

The Evaluator's Program Description (EPD) is a convenient format for recording and summarizing information about the goals of one or more programs, the activities to achieve the goals, and the evidence needed to prove that each goal has been achieved. An illustration of an EPD follows:

	Goals	Activities	Evidence of Program Merit
	(One by one, describe the goals each program is trying to achieve)	(For each goal, describe the program activities that will lead to the fulfillment of the goal)	(For each goal, describe the type of information that will be convincing evidence of program merit)

Goals and Activities (Columns 1 and 2 of the Evaluator's Program Description)

A program goal is a statement of intent. An activity is a means of achieving a goal. In completing the Evaluator's Program Description, the evaluator must describe one or more activities used to accomplish each goal. As an example, the goals and activities columns of an EPD could look like this:

EXAMPLE: THE EVALUATOR'S PROGRAM DESCRIPTION FOR A HEALTH EDUCATION PROGRAM

Goals	Activities	Evidence of Program Merit
1. To increase students' responsibility for their own health care	Special health curriculum materials emphasizing decision making are used. Classroom discussions by the school nurse or physician are conducted.	
2. XXX	XXX	

Because many programs lack clear and complete statements of their goals and activities, the relationships between goals and activities are often difficult to determine. Sometimes the evaluator must use experience and logic to extract clear and consistent goals and activities. Other times, the evaluator might recommend a formal needs assessment, a survey technique used to define program goals and to plan program activities. Many evaluators have trouble stating goals and activities that are neither too specific nor too general to use for evaluation purposes, but questions of specificity are more academic than actual. In practice, it is the complexity of the program that will determine how specific the statement of goals and activities should be. Some programs are really umbrellas for many smaller ones, each with its own philosophy and its own activities. ESEA Title 1 (compensatory education), for example, probably funds over 50,000 individual programs.

The evaluator's job in formulating program goals and activities is to state them so that:

- the important components of all programs and their underlying philosophies are represented
- each goal has one or more activities associated with it
- the priority of the goals is clear
- the resulting number of goals and activities is manageable for evaluation purposes.

Evidence of Program Merit (Column 3 of the Evaluator's Program Description)

In Column 3, the types of information that are acceptable as evidence of program merit should be summarized. A program has merit if it meets its goals, if the activities it uses to achieve its goals are beneficial, and if any unexpected effects of the program are positive. Actual evidence of a program's merit may be in the form of statements, events, objects, numbers, and observations. For example, in a program to improve reading skills, credible evidence of merit might include any or all of the following:

- a measured gain in students' reading skills
- an observed gain in students' reading skills
- testimony from students that their skills have improved
- testimony from parents that their children's skills have improved
- testimony from teachers that their students' skills have improved.

At least one indication of program merit must be identified for each program goal and each activity that is important to the client. For instance, in the health education program, evidence of program merit may take the forms shown in the following EPD.

EXAMPLE: THE EVALUATOR'S PROGRAM DESCRIPTION FOR A HEALTH EDUCATION PROGRAM

Goals	Activities	Evidence of Program Merit
1. To increase students' responsibility for their own health care	Special health curriculum materials emphasizing decision making are used. Classroom discussions by the school nurse or physician are conducted.	The use of special curriculum materials The conduct of classroom discussions by the school nurse or physician Testimony from nurses that students show a willingness to make decisions about their care when they have a health problem Students demonstrate significantly more understanding of the alternatives available in a medical emergency than they did at the beginning of the school year and more than comparable students who did not participate in the program
2. To XXX	XXX	XXX

The example shows four types of information required as evidence of program merit for the first goal and its activities. Curriculum materials must be available, classroom discussions must take place, nurses must give favorable testimony, and students must be able to demonstrate increased understanding.

The kind of information needed to prove the worth of a program should be decided cooperatively with the client in advance of the evaluation. Finding out what will convince a client of the program's merit is extremely important because it helps the evaluator to identify the information that must be produced, and it forces the client to be truthful and realistic about what he or she really wants to know about the program. Agreeing on evidence of program merit is an important safeguard because it protects the evaluator against claims that the findings are not relevant or not sufficient to prove the program's success or failure, and it protects the client against having the evaluator arbitrarily collect information claimed to be "good" or "important."

Reaching agreement about what constitutes evidence of a program's merit is one of the most difficult aspects of planning an evaluation. Few empirical or theoretical guidelines exist for establishing standards of achievement for educational, health, and social service programs. Questions such as "What is good mental health?" or "How much change in achievement must take place for a program to be considered educationally meaningful?" have no generally accepted answers. Often the evaluator and client have to reconcile what a local agency believes is meritorious about its program with what state or federal guidelines require as evidence of program success. For example, a local agency might define evidence of program merit in terms of the quality of its services and the effectiveness of its procedures, while the state or federal government might define evidence of program merit in terms of the number of people served, a program's cost effectiveness, and the way resources are allocated.

There are no easy solutions to the problems of identifying evidence of program merit. Sometimes the process means compromise; it always requires sensitivity to the social and political environment and to the client's needs.

Sources of Information for the EPD

In completing the EPD, the evaluator can consult the program documents, staff, and sponsors; the evaluation sponsor; and others concerned with and affected by the evaluation.

Written records of the program such as its proposal, earlier evaluation reports, and products or materials developed for and by the program comprise its documentation. Written documents are among the most useful, easily obtained, and least expensive sources of information for an evaluation of a developing program.

The program's staff includes its creators and the people who are responsible for its implementation. Consultation with staff is crucial when preparing an EPD for a new program to be sure that its goals, activities, and evidence of program merit are described accurately. Regardless of the program's age, however, it is probably advisable for the evaluator to enlist the help of program staff. They can provide valuable insight, and their involvement in planning the evaluation may make it easier to obtain their cooperation for later information collection activities.

The program's sponsors provide its financial support. They can be foundations, community groups, and local, state and federal agencies. Whenever possible, sponsors should be involved in the preparation of the EPD since they, too, can offer insights into the program. Their support can make the evaluation operation more efficient and lend credibility to the findings.

If the evaluation's sponsors and the program's sponsors are not the same, the evaluation's sponsors should be consulted separately. Their ideas about the program's goals and activities and their definitions of the program's merit may be very different from those in the program's documents or those held by the program's staff and sponsors. The evaluation's sponsors are especially important sources of information when performing an effectiveness evaluation since many program documents may not seem relevant or may be missing, and the original staff may no longer be involved in the program. Only the evaluation's sponsors may be attainable.

Other individuals or groups who may be affected by the program or its evaluation are the program participants and their families, advisory committees, and other citizens' groups. They can provide valuable information about the political and social atmosphere in which the program's goals and activities were created and those in which they currently exist.

A preliminary draft of the EPD should go to the client for review and amendments. Depending upon the purpose and size of the program, this document will undergo many changes before it will satisfy everyone. Sometimes it is enough for the evaluator to meet individually with the program director or the evaluation sponsor to come up with a description of the program that is adequate for evaluation purposes. In other cases the evaluator may be involved in a long series of meetings, starting with the program director and eventually including the program's staff and advisory committee, members of the local community and even people from the funding agency. The number of meetings and drafts of the EPD will vary, but the basic process is the same each time: the evaluator meets with a group of people to review and critique the most recent draft of the EPD, and then updates the EPD on the basis of their comments. Review meetings may be formal or informal, and often the "meeting" will be no more than a phone call or a brief note.

Once the evaluator has a complete description of the program's goals, activities, and evidence of merit, and the client has accepted that description as a basis for the evaluation, then the EPD is complete. The final version of the EPD should be made available to all who participated in its development.

A completed EPD for an effectiveness evaluation of a health education program for selected third-grade students appears on page 10.

The Evaluation Questions is a device for specifying all questions to be answered by the evaluation. These questions can take the following forms:

How well did the program achieve its goals?
Were the program's activities implemented as planned?
How effective were the activities in achieving the goals?
For which groups was the program most/least successful?
How did internal and external social and political factors influence the program's development and impact?
What social and political effects did the program have on the environment in which it was implemented?
What did the program cost?
How well was the program managed?
What are the merits of the program compared with alternative programs?

The evaluation questions that clients consider important will vary. In one evaluation the questions might be related to the program's goals and activities, while in another they might focus on costs. In any case, the number of questions that can be answered depends upon the client's priorities and the money, time, and resources available for evaluation.

The evaluation questions are the heart of the evaluation, and all activities

THE EVALUATION QUESTIONS (EQ)

EXAMPLE: THE EVALUATOR'S PROGRAM DESCRIPTION FOR A HEALTH EDUCATION PROGRAM

Goals	Activities	Evidence of Program Merit
1. To increase students' responsibility for their own health care	**Special health curriculum materials emphasizing decision making are used.** **Classroom discussions by the school nurse or physician are conducted.**	The use of special curriculum materials The conduct of classroom discussions by the school nurse or physician Testimony from nurses that students show a willingness to make decisions about their care when they have a health problem Students demonstrate significantly more understanding of the alternatives available to them in a medical emergency than they did at the beginning of the school year and more than comparable students who did not participate in the program
2. To increase students' knowledge about disease	**Special health curriculum materials emphasizing common adolescent and childhood diseases are used.**	The use of special curriculum materials Students demonstrate significantly more knowledge of diseases (i.e., their causes and symptoms, how they affect the body, and the ways in which they can be treated) than they did at the beginning of the program and more than comparable students who did not participate in the program An increase in the number of students who acquire the amount of knowledge considered to be acceptable for their grade level
3. To train school nurses and physicians, and teachers to teach self health care	**Inservice instruction is provided by the University's Continuing Education Department.**	Positive evaluation of the inservice training by teachers

must be organized so that they can be answered efficiently. Because of the importance of the questions, the client should agree to their selection and statement.

Sources of Information for the EQ

The main source of information for the EQ is the program merit column of the EPD, which defines successful accomplishment of a program's goals and activities. The evaluator can easily transform this information into questions about how well the goals were achieved, how successful the activities were and whether they were implemented as planned. For example, if the EPD for a continuing education program for teachers of bilingual students had as evidence of program merit (1) that lectures and practice sessions were held and (2) that teachers evaluated them positively, then the evaluator could transform this into the following evaluation questions:
* Did lectures and practice sessions take place?

- Did teachers consider them useful and enjoyable?

For many evaluations, particularly improvement evaluations with small budgets, all evaluation questions can be drawn directly from the EPD. Larger evaluations may want answers to additional questions. For example, for the continuing education program just mentioned, the following additional questions could also be asked:

- Which teachers profit most from the program, those with a Spanish heritage or those with another heritage?
- How effective would the program be if it were shortened by one day, thereby reducing the costs by 20%?

The evaluation questions are not the evaluator's questions. They are asked by those who commissioned the evaluation and who must use the evaluation information. Sometimes the client and evaluator have no trouble working together to arrive at the evaluation questions, and the client's cooperation is assured throughout. Sometimes some or all questions may have been chosen long before the evaluation, at the time of program planning. In this situation, the evaluator should check to be sure that the client still accepts the questions as important and that no new ones need to be added. Finally, the evaluation questions are sometimes mandated by law. The evaluator may add to them but must not substitute one question for another. For example, when Congress establishes a program, it often includes a requirement in the legislation calling for annual evaluations to determine how well the program's goals are being met. The evaluator for such a program would therefore be obligated to answer goal-attainment questions. At the request of the program's staff, the evaluator might also answer other questions, such as whether the goals changed over time, and whether any changes that occurred were meritorious.

Evaluation questions, it should be noted, are not immutable. Their purpose is to structure evaluations and not to restrict them. Some of the likely reasons for changing existing evaluation questions or adding new ones are that the program's goals and activities change (this can be expected primarily in improvement evaluations); the evaluator may uncover or suspect unintended consequences of participation in the program; or the client may develop new information needs as a result of preliminary evaluation information.

Because planning an evaluation is difficult, evaluators are sometimes tempted to work alone using only program documentation to prepare the EQ. Obtaining information from the program's staff and sponsors takes time and patience, but an evaluation is credible only if the evaluator considers the needs and perspectives of those who must interpret and apply its findings. Furthermore, evaluations are by nature political and social. That is, publication and use of findings can influence governments, institutions, and individuals to support or vilify programs, their sponsors, and participants.

Once a preliminary draft of the EQ is available, it should be sent to the client to:

- establish priorities for the questions
- add or delete questions
- check that all questions can be answered within the time period, given the resources available.

The number of questions and their specificity will be limited by the need to keep the evaluation manageable.

Sample evaluation questions for the health education program are given below. One set of questions is derived from the EPD (see the example on page 10), and one set of questions is based on considerations not specifically included in the EPD.

EXAMPLE: EVALUATION QUESTIONS FOR A
HEALTH EDUCATION PROGRAM

Questions based on the EPD

- Did students use special curriculum materials that emphasized decision making and common adolescent and childhood diseases?*

- Did the school nurse or physician conduct classroom discussions?

- Did nurses report that students were willing to make decisions about their care when they had a health problem?

- Did students understand significantly more about the alternatives available to them in a medical emergency at the end of the school year than they did at the beginning?

- Did students who participated in the program understand significantly more at the end of the school year than comparable students who did not participate?

- Did students know significantly more about diseases at the end of the school year than they did at the beginning?

- Did students who participated in the program know significantly more at the end of the school year than comparable students who did not participate?

- Did the number of students who acquired the amount of knowledge considered to be acceptable for their grade level increase?

- Did teachers positively evaluate their teaching?

Questions not specifically based on the EPD

- Which students (boys or girls, Anglos, Blacks, or Spanish heritage) benefited most or least from the program?

- How did this program compare with other health education programs in terms of its objectives, activities, and costs?

- What would be the benefit of increasing the program's funding per pupil by 20%?

---

*The tense of an evaluation question will vary according to the type of evaluation that is being conducted. Thus, in some improvement evaluations, this question might be phrased as: "Are students using special curriculum materials...?"

CHAPTER 3

CONSTRUCTING EVALUATION DESIGNS

A design strategy describes the ways in which people are grouped and variables are manipulated to answer one or more evaluation questions. In some evaluations a single design can be used to answer all questions, while in others several designs are required. A classic example of a design strategy is when people are separated into two groups and one group participates in an experimental program while the second participates in a placebo program.

Internal and external validity are the criteria evaluators use to decide how accurately the design strategy will provide answers to the evaluation questions. Internal validity means a design can distinguish between changes caused by the program being evaluated and those resulting from other sources. Campbell and Stanley* have identified seven factors that can threaten a design's internal validity because they may become confused with a program's influence. They are:

History If a program designed to change students' attitudes towards democracy coincided with a major event like the assassination of a president, then it would be difficult to determine whether any observed changes in attitude were due to the program or to the event. Historical threats are changes in the environment that occur at the same time as the program.

Maturation In a sex education program that made use of a factual test given at the beginning and end of the school year, it would be difficult to determine if any observed changes were due to the program or to the increased knowledge that often comes with age. Maturation threats are changes within the individuals participating in the program that result from natural biological or psychological development.

Ques. 4

Testing In an evaluation of a three-month mathematics program for which students took the same test before and after instruction, it is possible that any observed gains in learning were primarily due to the effects of taking a pretest rather than to the effects of the program. That is, the pretest gave students practice and made them so familiar with the test that their performance on the posttest could have improved even without the benefit of instruction. Testing threats are the effects of taking a pretest on subsequent posttests.

INTERNAL VALIDITY

---

*Campbell, Donald, T., & Stanley, Julian C., *Experimental and Quasi-Experimental Designs for Research*, Chicago, Rand McNally & Co., 1971.

Instrumentation For an evaluation of a teacher training program, participants' knowledge was measured by observers at the beginning and end of the program. Gains in learning could be attributed to the program, but they might also be linked to differences in the way the observations were conducted. Instrumentation threats are due to changes in the calibration of an instrument, or changes in the observers, scores, or the measuring instrument used from one time to the next.

Statistical regression It is a statistical fact that when people are chosen to participate in a program on the basis of their extremely high or low scores on some selection measure, the high scorers will perform less well and low scorers will perform better if they take the same or a similar test a second time. Consequently, if students are selected to participate in a program on the basis of their very low scores on a pretest, their average score on a similar posttest will probably increase whether or not the program has had any impact.

Selection To evaluate a program that rewarded students for attending school, the attendance records of participating and nonparticipating students were compared. If the two groups were not equivalent, it would be difficult to know whether any observed differences were due to the program or to inherent differences (like sex or ethnicity) between the students who did and did not participate. Selection threats result when assignment produces groups with innately different characteristics.

Mortality For an evaluation that compared a new asthma treatment with the traditional treatment, the 60 patients who volunteered for each group were asked to visit the clinic at the end of their treatment program for a mini-physical examination. Fifty-seven patients from the traditional group and 43 from the treatment group came for the examination, but the evaluator could not be sure if any changes in health status were the result of the treatment or the result of changes in the groups due to their differing drop-out rates. Mortality threats are the result of participants' dropping out of the evaluation.

EXTERNAL VALIDITY

External validity is the criterion for deciding whether the evaluation findings will hold true for other people in other places. Threats to external validity include:

Reactive effects of testing If a high protein weight reduction program required dieters to be weighed when they first enrolled in a program and every month thereafter, then it is possible that any weight losses would result primarily from participants' reaction to being weighed and then given a diet, rather than to the diet itself. Reactive effects of testing are threats that are due to a pretest sensitizing participants to a program.

Interactive effects of selection bias Even though a program was found to be effective for a certain kind of participant in one part of the country, it does not follow that the program is effective for a different kind of participant in another part of the country.

Reactive effects of innovation Participants may perform better simply because they are excited about taking part in an innovative program and/or an evaluation study. This phenomenon is also known as the Hawthorne effect.

Multiple program interference If an evaluation of a new theater arts program revealed that the same students were also in an experimental foreign language program, then it is possible that any observed changes in behavior were the product of the two programs in combination, and that they could not be reproduced if either was carried out independently.

All evaluation designs must be internally valid; otherwise it is impossible to have confidence in the accuracy of their findings. External validity is important whenever the findings are going to be applied to other people or other settings, as in most large programs, or when findings from current program participants are used to make decisions affecting future participants.

The evaluator should select a design strategy that controls for the most likely threats to validity. For example, an evaluator who decides that statistical regression is probably a more realistic threat to internal validity in a particular program than instrumentation should select a design that controls for statistical regression but not necessarily for instrumentation.

Three design strategies that pose differing threats to internal and external validity are the case design, time series, and comparison group designs.

CASE DESIGNS

A case design is used to examine a single, cohesive group. Evaluators typically use case designs to answer questions that ask for descriptions of a program's participants, goals, activities, and results. Questions about new or exemplary programs for which comparisons are not yet available almost always require case designs. Case designs have been used, for instance, to evaluate acupuncture clinics and alternative schools. Case designs are sometimes called "pre-experimental" since investigations using them can be conducted to establish the probable existence of certain outcomes, which if confirmed, can be studied in more controlled situations.

EXAMPLE: A CASE EVALUATION DESIGN

The State Department of Education decided to try an Equal Employment Program to help members of minorities and women expand their job opportunities. At the end of the year, evaluators were called in to answer questions about the job ranks of minority and female employees. To do this, the evaluators used a case design in which they interviewed all employees and reviewed employment records. The evaluation design is depicted in the following diagrams:

Sequence of Activities in Months:

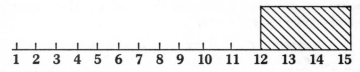

1 2 3 4 5 6 7 8 9 10 11 12 13 14 15

Program takes place during this time

Program is completed, but evaluation takes place during this time

Evaluation Design:

Program Participants

The most realistic threats to the internal validity of this case design are history (some event may occur at the same time as the program that changes employment opportunities); maturation (employees may change jobs naturally over the course of a year); instrumentation (with time the evaluator's interviewing style may change); and mortality (the people who remain employed and in the program may be inherently different from others who are fired or move away). The external validity of the design can be threatened by a Hawthorne effect (employees and employers may temporarily abandon their prejudices because of their interest in the program) and by the interactive effect of selection bias (there is no reason to assume that one state department's employees are the same as another's).

TIME SERIES DESIGNS

Time series designs involve repeatedly collecting information about the same group or groups over several periods of time. They are especially useful when an evaluation asks how a group's current performance compares with its past performance. An example of this is a longitudinal evaluation of educational achievement of students who participated in compensatory education programs. By comparing students' achievement from grade to grade, the extent and direction of changes can be determined. Time series designs can also be used to answer questions about how long a program's effects last. This might be done, for example, by testing students every year to find out how well they have retained knowledge each year for five years after they participated in the program. Time series designs help the evaluator guard against the possibility that unpredictable events, like losing records in a fire, will unduly influence the evaluation's findings. This design is frequently difficult to implement, however, because it is hard to keep track of program participants and staff over time. Most time series designs are referred to as quasi-experimental designs because they provide only partial control over threats to internal validity.

EXAMPLE: A TIME SERIES EVALUATION DESIGN

The State Department of Education is conducting an evaluation of elementary bilingual education programs funded by Title VII. The evaluation uses a time series design in which participating students who are currently in the fourth grade are tested on their attitudes and reading achievement twice a year for three years. The evaluation schedule and design look like this:

Measures at the end of	September Year 1	June Year 1	September Year 2	June Year 2	September Year 3	June Year 3

Program takes place during this time

The most realistic threats to the internal validity of the time series design in this example are history (some event that occurs at the same time as the program, like bilingual television, might change students' attitudes and reading achievement) and possibly instrumentation (if, for example, there were changes in the way the measures were calibrated from time to time). Testing and maturation can be ruled out as threats if it can be assumed that any shift occurring from Time 1 to Time 2 would occur from Time 2 to Time 3. Mortality is not a threat to internal validity if data from only those students

16

who participated in the entire program are interpreted. External validity is threatened by the reactive effects of testing (students may react to the measure and not to the program); the Hawthorne effect (students may learn because of their excitement about participating in an experimental program); the interactive effects of selection bias (due to a high drop out rate, the students who participate in the entire evaluation may not be representative of other fourth grade students); and multiple program interference (the students might also be involved in other programs sometime during the evaluation).

The strategy most often used to answer evaluation questions is the comparison group design. This design strategy divides people into two or more groups with one group participating in the program being evaluated. The others may take part in another program or may not participate in any program. In this example, the first group is called the experimental group and the second is called the control group. Some evaluation questions require a combination of time series and comparison group designs. If the various groups in a comparison group design are each measured several times, say bi-monthly for two years, then the design is both a time series design and a comparison group design.

Comparison group designs are frequently divided into two categories: "quasi-" and "true-" experimental designs. Both categories include comparison groups, but group membership is determined in different ways. In quasi-experimental designs, individuals are assigned to experimental and control groups in such a way that differences may exist between the groups before the program begins. Therefore, any observed differences between them after participation in the program cannot be conclusively linked to the experimental program. In true-experimental designs, on the other hand, assignment of individuals results in groups that are initially as similar as possible, and any observed differences can be linked to participation in the experimental program. In order to guarantee the similarity of the groups for a true-experimental design, it is usually necessary to assign individuals at random to various groups.

COMPARISON GROUP DESIGNS

EXAMPLE: A QUASI EXPERIMENTAL COMPARISON GROUP EVALUATION DESIGN
Part I

An evaluation was commissioned of three elementary school programs for hospitalized children. Parents could select the program of their choice for their eligible children. One of the questions addressed by the evaluation was whether parents were satisfied with their children's progress. To answer this question, parents in each group were asked to complete a questionnaire at the end of the school year. The evaluation design strategy for this question (a quasi-experimental comparison group design) can be depicted as:

Program 1	Program 2	Program 3

Part II

Another question posed for the evaluation of the three elementary school programs for hospitalized children was whether students' basic skills and achievement improved. To answer this question, students in each program were given the same achievement test three times: at the beginning of the school year, at the end of the first semester, and at the end of the school year. This evaluation design strategy (a quasi-experimental comparison group and time series design) can be depicted as:

	Program 1	Program 2	Program 3
Time 1			
Time 2			
Time 3			

The most likely threats to the internal validity of the quasi-experimental comparison group design used in the first part of this example are: (1) selection, because the students in the three groups may be different from one another at the beginning of the program (for example, parents of more severely ill children may have chosen one program over the others) and (2) mortality (children who did badly may have dropped out of one of the programs). History and maturation can be ruled out if they are likely to influence each group similarly and therefore cannot account for any differences among them. Testing and instrumentation are not threats because only one measure was administered. The design's external validity could be threatened by the Hawthorne effect; the interactive effects of selection bias (participating students may not be representative of all hospitalized children); or multiple program interference (the students might also be involved in other programs or activities that influence their progress).

The internal validity of the quasi-experimental comparison group and time series design in the second part of the example could be threatened by selection (since the students in the three groups could be different from one another at the beginning of the evaluation); testing (for example, the measure at the beginning of the year may give students practice in test-taking causing them to do better on the end-of-semester and end-of-year exams); and instrumentation (if there were changes in the way the test scores were computed from time to time). Mortality would not be a threat if only data from students who completed all three exams were analyzed. This design's external validity could be threatened by the reactive effects of testing (if the beginning of the year or mid-year tests influence students in one of the programs by acting as an instructional guide or motivator); by a Hawthorne effect (if students' excitement about the evaluation or the program influences them to improve their skills); by the interactive effects of selection bias (if students who participate in the evaluation are not representative of all hospitalized children); and by multiple program interference (if students are concurrently involved in another program to improve their achievement).

EXAMPLE: A TRUE EXPERIMENTAL
COMPARISON GROUP EVALUATION DESIGN
Part I

The Government commissioned an evaluation to determine which of three programs for blind children costs least. The evaluation used a comparison group design in which children at the Blair Institute were randomly assigned to one of the three programs, and the costs of the three programs were compared. The evaluation design is depicted in the following diagram:

	Program 1	Program 2	Program 3
All costs are measured at the conclusion of the programs			

Part II

Programs 1 and 2 proved to be equally cost-effective. The Government then commissioned an evaluation to determine which of these two programs provided the best learning experience. To answer this evaluation question, a comparison group design was selected in which achievement test scores from the beginning and end of the program for children in Programs 1 and 2 were compared. Here is a diagram of the evaluation design (a true experimental comparison group and a time series design):

	Time 1 (The beginning of the program)	Time 2 (The end of the program)
Program 1		
Program 2		

There are no realistic threats to the internal validity of the design used in the first part of the comparison group evaluation because children were randomly assigned to each program. Any factors that might be confused with the program's impact, like maturation or history, would affect all three groups equally. (If children had not been randomly assigned, then selection would be a threat to internal validity since it might interact with students' maturation, etc.) Its external validity, however, may be threatened because of the interactive effects of selection bias (the evaluation findings do not necessarily apply to blind children other than those at Blair Institute) and the Hawthorne effect (program administrators and staff may be thriftier than usual because they know the evaluaton involves comparing their program to its competitors).

The design used in the second part of the example is probably without threats to its internal validity. The threats to its external validity include the reactive effects of testing (the children may react to the tests more than to the programs); the interactive effects of selection bias (other blind children may not react to the program in the same way as the children at Blair Institute); and the Hawthorne effect (some children may perform better because they are excited about being involved in an innovative program).

SAMPLING

Closely associated with design strategies are the sampling procedures used to select people and assign them to groups. When an evaluation uses a case design, for example, sampling involves selecting people to be included in the study; when an evaluation uses a comparison design, sampling involves selecting people and then assigning them to various groups.

Sampling procedures vary in their complexity. Some are based on rules like "all men over 45 years of age are to be included." Others involve complicated mathematical algorithms to systematically produce a representative sample of a particular population.

Sampling also has implications for the way in which evaluation findings can

EXAMPLE: A SAMPLING PLAN

The Program

The University Health Center developed a new program to help people quit smoking. An evaluation was commissioned to determine the program's effectiveness with male and female undergraduates of different ages. The evaluation used a comparison group design in which the program was compared to the Health Center's traditional Quit Smoking Program, taking into account participants' age and sex. The evaluation design is shown in the following diagram:

	Undergraduates 16-20 Years of Age		Undergraduates 21-25 Years of Age	
	Men	Women	Men	Women
New Program				
Traditional Program				

Selecting Students to Be Included in the Evaluation

Three hundred and ten undergraduates signed up for the Health Center's Quit Smoking Program for the winter semester. Of these, 140 were students between 16 and 20 years of age, of which 62 were men and 78 were women. There were 170 students between 21 and 25 years of age, of which 80 were men and 90 were women. All 310 undergraduates were selected to participate in the evaluation.

Assigning Students to the New and Traditional Programs

Participants in the evaluation were assigned to the new and traditional programs using a random stratified sampling procedure in which:

- the 62 men between 16 and 20 years were randomly assigned to the new or traditional program
- the 78 women between 16 and 20 years were randomly assigned to the new or traditional program
- the 80 men between 21 and 25 years were randomly assigned to the new or traditional program
- the 90 women between 21 and 25 years were randomly assigned to the new or traditional program

Using this sampling plan, the number of undergraduates placed in each category of the evaluation design is shown below.

	Undergraduates 16-20 Years of Age		Undergraduates 21-25 Years of Age	
	Men	Women	Men	Women
New Program	31	39	40	45
Traditional Program	31	39	40	45

be interpreted. Consider a case design used in an evaluation of a weight reduction program in which all participants are volunteers. Since the participants are volunteers and have not been selected in any systematic manner, the evaluation findings probably could not be generalized to other groups. This is because there is no way of knowing whether some special self-selecting factor, like doctor's orders, prompted people to join the group, thereby making them different from other dieters.

Evaluators are frequently required to select a sample that is representative of all participants in the program being evaluated. A representative sample is a miniature version of the population to which the evaluation's findings can be applied. Three methods for obtaining representative samples are:

1. **Simple random sampling.** The total population is considered to be a single group and from it the appropriate number of people is randomly selected. For example, a lottery system could be used to select 10 hospitals from all hospitals in a state.

2. **Stratified random sampling.** The total population is divided into subgroups (like males and females), and then from each group a certain number of people is randomly selected so that their number in the sample is proportionate to the subgroup's size in the total population. For example, if there are twice as many men as women, in order to obtain a representative sample of 120 people, 80 men would be randomly selected from all men and 40 women would be selected from all women.

Simple and stratified random sampling techniques are the most accurate means of creating the similar or equivalent comparison groups that are necessary for true-experimental design strategies.

3. **Purposive sampling.** Individuals or groups are deliberately selected for a particular reason. For example, a joint committee of teachers and administrators might decide that a representative sample of a program's participants should include one gifted classroom, three regular classrooms, and one classroom of slow learners.

No matter what sampling technique is used, it is always necessary to compare the sample to the total population in terms of relevant factors such as ethnic composition, socioeconomic status, and achievement levels.

INDEPENDENT AND DEPENDENT VARIABLES

Independent variables form the structure of a design and are the factors that are manipulated in an evaluation. Dependent variables are the factors that are observed and measured to determine the results of manipulating the independent variables. For example, if an evaluation question asks about the effects on student achievement of reducing the number of students in a classroom from 20 to 30, then the independent variable is the number of students in the classroom and the dependent variable is student achievement. In this example, the independent variable is studied at two levels: 30 students and 20 students per classroom.

For the first part of the comparison group example on page 19 (comparing costs of three programs for blind children) the independent variable is the program and it is being studied at three levels: Programs 1, 2, and 3. The dependent variable is a measure of program costs.

THE EVALUATION DESIGN DESCRIPTION

The Evaluation Design Description (EDD) is a convenient way to summarize information about the design strategies selected for an evaluation. For each evaluation question, the EDD specifies the type of design strategy, the independent and dependent variables, the sampling procedures, and the threats to internal and external validity. In addition, the EDD offers a graphic picture of the design strategy chosen for each evaluation question.

As an example, an excerpted EDD for the health education program follows.

EXAMPLE: EXCERPTED EVALUATION DESCRIPTION FOR A HEALTH EDUCATION PROGRAM

Design Strategy

Evaluation Questions	Type	Pictorial Representation	Independent Variables	Dependent Variables	Sampling	Threats to Validity
Did students who participated in the program know significantly more about diseases at the end of the school year than comparable students who did not participate?	Comparison group (with time series) design	Experimental Program / Control Program; Pre / Post	The program (which is being studied at two levels: experimental and control) Timing of measures (which is being studied at two levels: before and after instruction) Note: This variable can also be considered a covariate.	Knowledge of diseases	One third-grade classroom from each participating school is randomly selected for the experimental program, and one classroom from each school is randomly selected to constitute the non-participant group	External Validity: • Reactive effects of testing • Interactive effects of selection bias • Reactive effects of innovation • Multiple program interference (?)
Did the number of students who acquired the amount of knowledge considered to be acceptable for their grade level increase?	Time series design	Pre / Post	Timing of measures (which is being studied at two levels: before and after instruction)	Knowledge of diseases	All classrooms that are randomly selected to participate in the experimental program will be included in this design	Internal Validity: • History • Maturation (?) • Testing (?) • Instrumentation (?) External Validity: • Reactive effects of testing • Interactive effects of selection bias • Reactive effects of innovation • Multiple program interference

Evaluation question	Design	Timing of measures	Variables	Sampling	Threats to validity
riculum materials that emphasized decision making and common adolescent and childhood diseases?			materials	selected to participate in the experimental program will be included in this evaluation design	• Maturation • Instrumentation • Mortality External Validity: • Interactive effects of selection bias • Reactive effects of innovation • Multiple program interference (?)
Did students know significantly more about diseases at the end of the school year than they did at the beginning?	Time series design	Pre / Post	Timing of measures (which is being studied at two levels: before and after instruction)	Knowledge of diseases	All classrooms that are randomly selected to participate in the experimental program will be included in this evaluation design	Internal Validity: • History • Maturation (?) • Testing (?) • Instrumentation (?) External Validity: • Reactive effects of testing • Interactive effects of selection bias • Reactive effects of innovation • Multiple program interference (?)
Which students (boys or girls, Anglo, Black, or Spanish Heritage) benefited most/least from the program?	Comparison group (with time series) design	Pre / Post — Anglo Boys/Girls, Black Boys/Girls, Spanish Boys/Girls	Students' sex (which is being studied at two levels: boys and girls) Students' ethnicity (which is being studied at three levels: Anglo, Black, and Spanish Heritage) Timing of measures (which is being studied at two levels: before and after instruction)	Benefit from the program (to be derived from achievement scores and interview information)	All classrooms that are randomly selected to participate in the experimental program will be included in this evaluation design	Internal Validity: • Selection External Validity: • Reactive effects of testing • Interactive effects of selection bias • Reactive effects of innovation • Multiple program interference (?)

CHAPTER 4

PLANNING INFORMATION COLLECTION

Planning information collection for an evaluation requires finding the most efficient techniques to answer questions about a program's merit, setting the time and place for gathering information, and deciding who will participate in the evaluation and be responsible for the collection of data.

TECHNIQUES USED TO COLLECT INFORMATION

Many information collection techniques can be used to answer evaluation questions. Consider the following excerpt from an Evaluator's Program Description and the corresponding evaluation question:

Goals	Activities	Evidence of Program Merit
To improve students' reading ability	The XYZ reading program is used for 15 minutes each day for one semester.	• Improvement is reported by teachers, parents, and students. • Students' reading scores improve from the beginning to the end of the school year.

Evaluation Question: How much have students' reading skills improved?

To provide a credible answer to this question, the evaluator could use any of the following information collection techniques:
1. Give parents a rating scale to assess their children's reading performance.
2. Send questionnaires to teachers to get their opinions about students' reading performance.
3. Interview students to ask their opinions about their own reading performance.
4. Observe students as they read, and rate their reading ability.

5. Have students keep a diary of their progress.
6. Give students a nationally normed achievement test that assesses reading performance.
7. Have students take a teacher-developed reading test.
8. Review students' records for achievement test scores, report card grades, and teachers' comments.

As this list illustrates, the evaluator may choose among six techniques to answer the question about improved reading skills: interviews, questionnaires, rating scales, observations, record reviews, and achievement tests. To choose the best, consider the following factors:

First, the client should be satisfied. If an evaluator wants to use questionnaires but the client prefers interviews, the evaluator must decide just how serious the consequences of imposing an unwanted technique might be. Second, the information collection techniques should be technically sound and the data collected from them should be reliable, valid, and targeted to the evaluation questions. Third, the information collection techniques should provide the best data the evaluation budget can afford, which means that the evaluator will have to decide such things as whether to buy or to develop measures and whether to use one or more techniques for each evaluation question. Fourth, the evaluator should choose techniques that allow enough time to gather and analyze data.

Sometimes the evaluator will have to negotiate with the client. Suppose a client wanted to use a test that had been proven unreliable in comparable situations. Then it is the evaluator's responsibility to explain the problem, suggest alternative solutions, and help the client reach a decision.

Different techniques are often used together to collect information to answer the same evaluation question. This is a good idea for variables that are hard to measure like attitudes, values, and beliefs because many sources of information are necessary to get at the truth. But the evaluator must be careful not to abuse this multi-measure approach because it can result in a mass of unmanageable data that are extremely costly to read, interpret, and analyze.

Just as several techniques may be useful to collect information about one aspect of an evaluation, so one information collection technique can sometimes be used to answer several evaluation questions. For example, a single questionnaire could be developed to obtain information about such diverse factors as a program's administrative problems, the education of its staff, and its impact on the community.

Classification of Information Collection Techniques

Major techniques for information collection are: performance tests, rating and ranking scales, archive reviews, observations, interviews, questionnaires, and achievement tests.

Performance Tests

Performance tests involve having an individual or group perform an activity or task and making an assessment of the quality of the performance. Examples of performance tests include having an individual type a letter, then counting the number of words typed correctly in a set amount of time, or having a group of experts observe a teacher instruct a class and then appraising the teacher's ability to instruct, using a rating scale specially designed for the purpose. The major advantage of performance testing is that it relies on tasks that are close to "real world" activities. Its major disadvantages are that it is usually very time consuming and expensive. The following example is an overview of a performance test in which an individual is given 25 minutes to teach a lesson about test validity. Teachers are given the objective for their lesson, a question typical of the test items that will be given to students, and background information to help them teach. At the conclusion of the lesson, students take a test to see whether they have learned what was intended. A teacher is considered successful if student scores are high.

EXAMPLE: OVERVIEW OF A PERFORMANCE TEST

Instructional Objective:

The student will identify the basic characteristics of content, concurrent, predictive, and construct validity.

Sample Test Item:

The construct validity of a test is established by:

- **A. Comparing test scores to a teacher's evaluation of the students' standings relative to the construct**
- **B. Devising a second test to cover the same construct and comparing the two sets of scores**
- **C. Comparing performance on each item with the overall test score**
- ***D. Using the test to experimentally verify the construct on which the test is based**

Intended Learners: **Teachers; school administrators; curriculum and instruction personnel; test and measurement specialists.**

Time Allotted for Instruction: **25 minutes**

Background Information: **See accompanying materials on the following pages.**

Rating and Ranking Scales

Rating and ranking scales can be used for self assessment or to assess other people, events, or products on a given dimension. A numerical score is obtained for each thing that is judged. Students' attentiveness, for example, can be rated on a five-point scale from 1="not very attentive" to 5="very attentive." Asking a teacher to rank four textbooks from one to four according to preference is an example of a ranking scale. The advantages of rating and ranking scales are that they are relatively inexpensive to construct, they are usually easily understood, and the information they provide readily lends itself to analysis. The disadvantage is that they are subject to many types of bias. Some raters are lenient and others are not; some base their ratings on personal feelings; and sometimes raters are asked to make distinctions (especially when ranking) when they do not perceive any differences. Examples of ranking and rating scales follow.

EXAMPLE: EXCERPT FROM A RANKING SCALE

The list below contains five purposes of preschool educa-tion. Please rank these purposes according to how much emphasis each received in your State Preschool Program during the last school year. The purpose that is emphasized

most should be ranked "1," the second most emphasized should be ranked "2," etc. Be sure to write in a rank for each purpose.

PRESCHOOL PURPOSE	RANK
To help children improve their visual and hearing sensitivity; to facilitate muscle development and coordination	
To help children develop skills in communication verbally and orally; to promote ability to deal with concepts such as number, time, color, and size	
To help children become considerate of others, cooperative and friendly; to help them want to share, and to respect public and private property	
To help children acquire a favorable attitude toward attending school, their teachers and learning; to help promote an appreciation of persistence and achievement	
To help children develop a healthy self-concept, self-esteem, and self-confidence; to develop a sense of personal worth, self-understanding and security	

EXAMPLE: EXCERPT FROM A RATING SCALE

The following statements are objectives or services of family practice medical programs throughout the country. Please respond to each statement by indicating how important it is to you.

Objectives of Family Practice Medical Programs	LEAST IMPORTANT (1)	BELOW AVERAGE IMPORTANCE (2)	AVERAGE IMPORTANCE (3)	ABOVE AVERAGE IMPORTANCE (4)	MOST IMPORTANT (5)
1. To let people know what kinds of health services are available to them (e.g., they can come for physical exams and checkups without being sick; they can come for screening for sugar diabetes, blood pressure, sickle cell anemia)					
2. To teach individuals and families about common health problems (e.g., lead poisoning, high blood pressure, overweight)					
3. To help get people to a physician or hospital when they need one, such as in an emergency					
4. To set up health care services in the community that are close to the people					
5. To reduce the cost of a visit to a clinic or a doctor's office					

Archive Reviews   Archive reviews refer to collecting evaluation information from program-related documents. In a program where upper-elementary pupils serve as tutors to lower-grade pupils, for example, the evaluator could review attendance records to determine whether the tutors or the youngsters they instruct came to school more regularly after the program began. Another example of the use of archive reviews is abstracting information from patients' medical records to find out how accurately physicians made diagnoses and followed appropriate procedures. The advantages of archive reviews are that they do not interfere with the program being evaluated and that they are relatively inexpensive. Their disadvantages include legal problems associated with obtaining and using records, and the possibility that program documents may be disorganized or unavailable. Illustrations of archive review forms follow.

EXAMPLE: AN ARCHIVE REVIEW FORM FOR SCHOOL RECORDS

School Code: _____

State: _____

Grade Level(s): _____

Teacher Code: _____

Total No. Days, Fall '7X Semester: _____

Programs
(check all that apply)

Title I _____

Title III _____

Title VII _____

Other _____

Student ID	No. Days Absent Fall '7X Semester	Birthdate Mo/Day/Yr	Sex B=Boy G=Girl	Ethnic Group A=Asian B=Black H=Hispanic W=White O=Other	Fall Test Scores			
					Listen-ing	Mathe-matics	Read-ing	Total

EXAMPLE: AN ARCHIVE REVIEW FORM FOR A MEDICAL CHART AUDIT

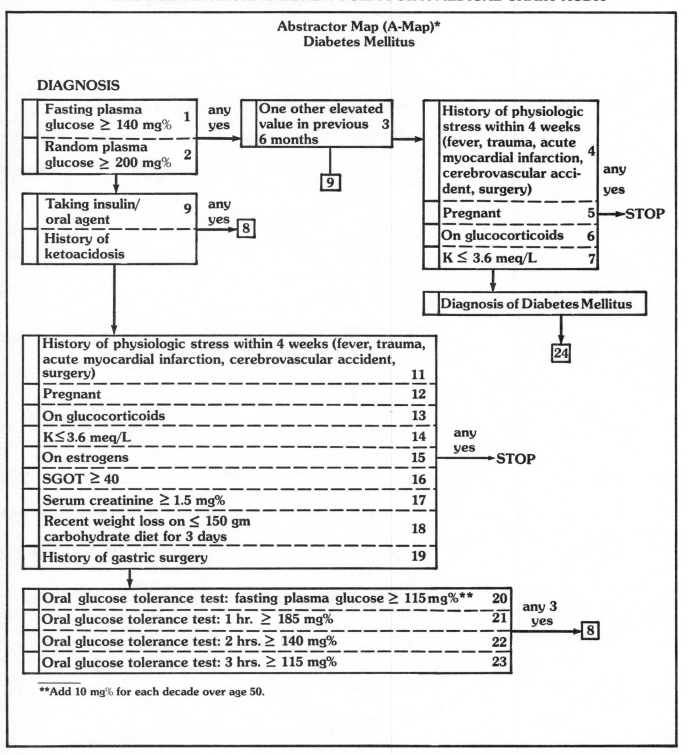

Abstractor Map (A-Map)*
Diabetes Mellitus

DIAGNOSIS

Fasting plasma glucose ≥ 140 mg% **1**	
Random plasma glucose ≥ 200 mg% **2**	

any yes →

| One other elevated value in previous **3** 6 months | |

9

| History of physiologic stress within 4 weeks (fever, trauma, acute myocardial infarction, cerebrovascular accident, surgery) **4** | |
| Pregnant **5** |
| On glucocorticoids **6** |
| K ≤ 3.6 meq/L **7** |

any yes → STOP

| Taking insulin/ oral agent **9** |
| History of ketoacidosis |

any yes → **8**

Diagnosis of Diabetes Mellitus

24

| History of physiologic stress within 4 weeks (fever, trauma, acute myocardial infarction, cerebrovascular accident, surgery) **11** |
| Pregnant **12** |
| On glucocorticoids **13** |
| K ≤ 3.6 meq/L **14** |
| On estrogens **15** |
| SGOT ≥ 40 **16** |
| Serum creatinine ≥ 1.5 mg% **17** |
| Recent weight loss on ≤ 150 gm carbohydrate diet for 3 days **18** |
| History of gastric surgery **19** |

any yes → STOP

| Oral glucose tolerance test: fasting plasma glucose ≥ 115 mg%** **20** |
| Oral glucose tolerance test: 1 hr. ≥ 185 mg% **21** |
| Oral glucose tolerance test: 2 hrs. ≥ 140 mg% **22** |
| Oral glucose tolerance test: 3 hrs. ≥ 115 mg% **23** |

any 3 yes → **8**

**Add 10 mg% for each decade over age 50.

Observations

Another information collection technique involves observation of individuals or program activities. The information collected by observers can be reported by checklists, rating scales, field notes, and summary reports. In a work-training program, for example, observations might be used to determine if training is taking place according to plan. The advantages of observations are that they help the information collectors become familiar with and sensitive to the program, and that they are often the only feasible and economical way to gather certain kinds of information. The disadvantages of this technique are that it is costly to train information collectors, that the people being observed may not behave normally because of the presence of the information collector, and that several observations may be needed to get reliable (i.e., consistent) results. Sample items from an observation form are given below.

EXAMPLE: SAMPLE ITEMS FROM AN OBSERVATION FORM

I. *Your estimate of the audience's*
  1. Size
    _____ Fewer than 50
    _____ 51-100 persons
    _____ 100 or more
  2. Sex
    _____ % male   _____ % female

  3. Age
    _____ % less than 20 years
    _____ % 21-35 years
    _____ % 36-50 years
    _____ % 51 or more years

II. *Discussion*
    _____ 1. How many different people asked questions?
    _____ 2. How many people left before the discussion ended?
    _____ 3. How many times did the discussion leader refer to the film?

Interviews

An interview is an information collection technique in which a person talks with another person or group. The information gathered can be recorded on field notes, structured interview forms, summary reports, or other related forms. Interviews can be completely unstructured and spontaneous, or questions can be predetermined, or questions and response categories can be decided ahead. Interviews might be used, for example, to find out why participants dropped out of a program, and might consist of several key questions with a series of follow-up questions for each. The major advantage of interviews is that they permit in-depth probes of sensitive subjects like attitudes or values. Their primary disadvantages are that they are usually time consuming and costly, and that interviewers must be specially trained. An illustration of interview questions is given below.

EXAMPLE: SAMPLE INTERVIEW QUESTIONS

How do you determine how well your students are reading?
  PROBE: Tests? Diagnostic procedures? Informal measures?
        How often used?

30

What do you do about students who do not seem to be learning from reading instruction?

PROBE: What kinds of difficulties were there? Did you have materials and other resources?

Do you involve parents in any way in the classroom?

PROBE: How? Why not?

Questionnaires

Questionnaires are self-administered survey forms that consist of a set of questions. Rating and ranking scales are frequently used in questionnaires. Answers to questionnaire items can require free responses (e.g., short answers) or can be structured into "forced" choices (e.g., multiple choice). Questionnaires are used frequently in large-scale evaluations to obtain participants' reactions and opinions. The major advantages of questionnaires are that they are less expensive to construct than most measures, and the resulting information is relatively easy to analyze. Their major disadvantage is that when the questions and/or the response categories are already drawn up, the kind of information obtained is limited. An excerpt from a questionnaire follows.

EXAMPLE: EXCERPT FROM A QUESTIONNAIRE

1. *Please rate the cook-to-order grill in your dormitory.*

	Definitely Yes		No Opinion		Definitely No
a. Cook-to-order food is better tasting than regular dorm food.	5	4	3	2	1
b. You can get rare, medium or well-done dishes upon request.	5	4	3	2	1
c. The service is fast and efficient.	5	4	3	2	1

2. *How did you form your opinion of the cook-to-order grill? (Check one)*
    _____ 1. I eat at the grill at least once a week.
    _____ 2. I eat at the grill at least once a month.
    _____ 3. I eat at the grill at least once a quarter.
    _____ 4. I have not eaten at the grill but have heard about it from others.
3. *What might be done to improve the cook-to-order grill in your dorm?*

Achievement Tests

Achievement tests are pencil and paper measures of competence in a given subject matter. Achievement tests can be developed by the program or evaluation staff, or they can be purchased from publishers. Achievement tests can be used for such things as measuring a student's knowledge of basic

English usage or a pharmacist's knowledge of reactions caused by commonly prescribed drugs. The advantage of achievement tests is that they can be administered to large groups at relatively low costs. One disadvantage is that the tests must be properly validated to ensure their accuracy. Further, having high scores on a test of factual knowledge does not necessarily mean that the knowledge can be applied. An excerpt from an achievement test containing two multiple-choice items and one essay question is given below.

EXAMPLE: EXCERPTS FROM AN ACHIEVEMENT TEST

Multiple choice:

1. Wanted: School counselor, must have Master's Degree or equivalent; administrative experience desirable but not necessary; must be able to relate to students.

   Is the above job description sex stereotyped?

   A. Yes, a female stereotype.

   B. Yes, a male stereotype.

   *C. No, there is no stereotype.

2. Which of the following statements is the best example of sex stereotyping?

   A. Film producers are very rich.

   *B. Nurses are motherly.

   C. Plumbers can usually drive a truck.

   D. Mathematicians can solve multiplication problems in their heads.

3. Essay:

   Briefly describe the provisions of Title IX of the Education Amendments and explain how they might apply to you.

Structured-Response Versus Free-Response Formats

Information collection techniques can use either a structured-response format in which an answer is selected from a set of already provided responses, or a free-response format in which the respondent develops an answer. A multiple choice test item is an example of a structured-response format, and an essay question is an example of a free-response format. The major advantage of structured responses is the ease in scoring them, resulting in a more accurate and reliable score. Free responses are usually used when it is impossible to anticipate the range of responses in advance. In general, structured responses are recommended for obtaining objective kinds of information and for large-scale information collection activities. Free responses are recommended for small, in-depth information collection activities and for obtaining information about opinions and ideas.

---

*Correct answer.

Information collection techniques can also be designed to use either subjective or objective scoring procedures. Subjective procedures rely heavily on the interpretations of individuals actually doing the scoring. Objective procedures do not rely on individual judgments, but on rules that all scorers can apply in precisely the same way. An example of objective scoring is using an answer key for a multiple choice test and an example of subjective scoring is assigning grades of A to F to an essay test based on the scorers' judgment. The major advantages of subjective information collection techniques are that they are relatively easy to construct and they allow a person to respond in his or her own words. The major advantages of objective techniques are their ease of scoring and their reliability. Subjective techniques are best for gathering personal or sensitive information in small-scale evaluations where just a few persons can score all responses, while objective techniques are best for large-scale evaluations with many information collectors working independently.

Objective Versus Subjective Scoring

A norm-referenced test permits scores to be translated into percentiles and stanines, automatically allowing comparisons of individuals or groups. Criterion-referenced tests provide scores like "number of test items correct for each objective" and "mastery levels," which represent how well individuals or groups have acquired certain abilities and knowledge. Examples of norm-referenced tests are college entrance examinations and medical school qualification examinations. One example of a criterion-referenced test is a typing test, where 60 error-free words per minute are required as evidence of secretarial skill. Other examples are competency-based tests used to recertify paramedics and to license teachers.

Neither type of test has any inherent advantage over the other. If an evaluation question calls for comparative data, then a test with norm-referenced score interpretations should be used; but if descriptive information or minimum performance standards are involved, then a test with criterion-referenced score interpretations should be used. Many evaluations require both norm- and criterion-referenced score interpretations. "Did students in our program do better than students in the alternative program and did they meet the minimum standards of performance?" is an evaluation question that calls for interpreting scores in both ways.

Norm- Versus Criterion-Referenced Tests

Selecting an instrument for collecting information involves reviewing currently available measures and then choosing or adapting the most appropriate one. Sometimes a new instrument must be developed. The decision to select, adapt, or develop information collection instruments can become complex, and the advantages and disadvantages of each must be carefully considered.

SELECTING, ADAPTING, OR DEVELOPING THE RIGHT INSTRUMENT FOR INFORMATION COLLECTION

Selecting Already Developed Information Collection Instruments

A major advantage in selecting an existing information collection instrument is that it is less expensive than developing a new one or adapting one from several sources. Further, if the instrument has been used effectively at least once before in a similar evaluation situation, the evaluator may have some confidence in its applicability to the present evaluation. Finally, some instruments have the additional advantage of being validated through expert review and field testing. This provides the evaluator with documentation describing the conditions under which the instrument may be used with confidence.

There are also disadvantages in selecting already developed instruments. First, they may be hard to find and the search can be time consuming. Second, the instruments that are available may not provide the best information to answer the evaluation questions. Third, just because it exists and has been used does not mean that an instrument has been reviewed or systematically tested to determine its validity. Even a validated instrument may have been tested for use in situations that are totally unlike those of the present evaluation.

An already-developed instrument is often a good choice when the evaluation is measuring general ability and knowledge, or difficult-to-measure psychological states like hostility. Much time, money, and expertise have been devoted to developing and validating intelligence tests and qualifying examinations.

Adapting Information Collection Instruments

Adapting already developed instruments enables the evaluator to combine the features of several instruments. Adaptation can also have the advantage of saving the time and money it takes to develop an instrument. Among the disadvantages of adaptation are the difficulty in finding appropriate instruments, the possibility of having to validate the hybrid that results from combining parts of various instruments, and potential problems in obtaining permission to adapt all or part of someone else's instruments. It is a good choice when there are several validated instruments that together meet the evaluation's needs.

Developing Information Collection Instruments

Designing an instrument is the best guarantee for getting the needed evaluation information, but it requires considerable skill and time. It can also be expensive because subject matter experts or psychometricians sometimes need to be consulted and because new instruments have to be validated. When opinions and factual data must be obtained through interviews and questionnaire surveys, it is usually more efficient to develop new instruments than to find or adapt existing ones.

PREPARING INFORMATION COLLECTION FORMS

Two forms, the Evaluation Questions with the Information Collection Techniques (EQ with ICT) and the Information Collection Plan (ICP) can be used to organize information collection. An illustration of these forms appears below.

THE EVALUATION QUESTIONS WITH INFORMATION COLLECTION TECHNIQUES

Evaluation Questions	Information Collection Techniques to Be Used	Limitations			
		Schedule	Design	Sampling	Other

INFORMATION COLLECTION PLAN

Specific Information Collection Techniques (Instruments)	Time and Place for Information Collection	Nature of the Sample for the Technique	Who Will Collect the Information

The EQ with ICT is a form for organizing information collection to ensure that each evaluation question will be answered. Each evaluation question is listed on the form along with the information collection techniques that will be used and a list of any limitations imposed by the evaluation's schedule, design, or sampling procedures.

The first step in developing the EQ with ICT is to take each evaluation question and match it with an appropriate information collection technique. How many and which techniques should be used for each question depends upon their acceptability to the client and their technical soundness and efficiency in providing timely information.

Next the evaluator should note the limitations on the use of each technique caused by scheduling, design strategy and sampling procedures. Limitations on information collection can be imposed by the schedules of the people involved in the evaluation or by report deadlines. For example, evaluations of inoculation programs for students in western states like California, New Mexico, and Texas are limited by the fact that many students in those states are children of migrant farm workers who do not start school until late October. Consequently, the evaluator must wait until late November to visit schools. The design strategy can also impose limitations and these should be recorded on the EQ with ICT. For instance, an evaluation that uses a time series design with an achievement test scheduled immediately before, immediately after, and six months after the program is limited because the evaluator may have to develop three parallel test forms for the achievement test. The evaluator should also note on the EQ with ICT any special limitations on information collection resulting from the sampling procedures. If all participants, rather than a sample of participants, must take a performance test at the conclusion of a program, for example, that imposes a special limitation on the evaluator's schedule and budget. Finally, any special circumstances that may affect information collection should be recorded on the EQ with ICT. These might include limited access to data in personal records and official clearance requirements for questionnaires and interview schedules.

Developing the Evaluation Questions with the Information Collection Techniques Form

As a third step in completing the EQ with ICT, the evaluator should meet with the client and review the draft, calling special attention to any limitations cited. This is the time when selection of information collection techniques can be negotiated. For example, the client who wants face-to-face interviews with all participants might be persuaded that budget realities make it more practical to use group interviews or telephone interviews with a small sample of the participants and a questionnaire survey of the remaining participants.

Once the evaluator and the client have reached agreement, the fourth step for the evaluator is to review the EQ with ICT document to see whether some information collection techniques can be combined to answer several evaluation questions. For example, if interviews have been selected as the best way to get information for five evaluation questions, these could be combined so that one set of interviews will provide information to answer all five questions. The following is an excerpt from an EQ with ICT for a health education program.

EXAMPLE: EXCERPTED EVALUATION QUESTIONS WITH INFORMATION COLLECTION TECHNIQUES FOR A HEALTH EDUCATION PROGRAM

Evaluation Questions	Information Collection Techniques to Be Used	Limitations			
		Schedule	Design	Sampling	Other
Did students use special curriculum materials that emphasized decision making and common adolescent and childhood diseases?	Archive review of curriculum materials				
Did nurses report that students were willing to make decisions about their care when they had a health problem?	Interview with nurses	Nurses cannot be interviewed when students are waiting to see them.			
Did students know significantly more about diseases at the end of the school year than they did at the beginning?	Achievement test		Must have parallel forms of the achievement test.	All program participants must be tested.	Must ensure confidentiality of responses.
Did students who participated in the program know significantly more about diseases at the end of the school year than comparable students who did not participate?	Achievement test			All program participants must be tested.	Must ensure confidentiality of responses.
Did the number of students who acquired the amount of knowledge considered to be acceptable for their grade level increase?	Achievement test		Some schools are nongraded, and it is therefore difficult to designate some students by traditional grade levels.		Need criteria for acceptable knowledge at given grade levels.
Did teachers positively evaluate their training?	Teacher questionnaires				
Which students (boys or girls, Blacks, Anglos, or Spanish heritage) benefited most/least from the program?	Achievement tests Interviews with nurses			Some schools may not keep records of students' ethnicities.	Must develop an index for measuring benefit from the program.

36

The ICP is a planning document for describing how each information collection technique will be used. It is organized by specific techniques or instruments.

The first step in developing the ICP is to name each separate information collection technique. For example, suppose an EQ with ICT lists two achievement tests and three observations, and the evaluator has decided to combine the observations into one checklist. Then, in completing the ICP, the evaluator must decide which specific observation checklist and achievement tests to use (for example, the ABC and XYZ standardized achievement tests and an evaluator-developed observation form). Next, the evaluator must record on the ICP when and where each instrument will be administered, to whom, and by whom. Will some information collection methods be used more than once? How long will it take to complete the activity? Where will the information collection take place? The answers to all these questions should be included on the ICP.

The evaluator must record on the ICP whether information will be collected from all participants or only some. If only some individuals are going to be sampled, they should be identified. For example, the evaluator may choose to send questionnaires to all participants, but may plan to interview only 10% of them.

Finally, the evaluator should record on the ICP who will collect the information. For example, the evaluation team may collect the information, or the evaluator may decide to hire information collectors or train members of the program staff to collect the information.

Once the ICP is complete, the client should review and approve it. The following example is an excerpt from an ICP for a health education program.

Developing the Information Collection Plan

EXAMPLE: EXCERPTED INFORMATION COLLECTION PLAN FOR A HEALTH EDUCATION PROGRAM

Specific Information Collection Techniques (Instruments)	Time and Place for Information Collection	Nature of the Sample for the Technique	Who Will Collect the Information
Archive review of curriculum materials*	At the beginning of each semester at the school	All curriculum materials being used and all participating third-grade students	The evaluation team will review curriculum documents with the assistance of a curriculum consultant.
Interview with nurses*	The first two weeks of October and May in the student health center	All nurses in the school district	The evaluation team will conduct the interviews.
The New Health Achievement Test: Forms A and B	The first week in October and the last week in May in students' regular classrooms	All students in third-grade classrooms receiving the program, and all students in third-grade classrooms selected not to receive any program	Teachers will be trained to administer the tests, and the evaluation team will monitor the process.
Teacher questionnaires*	At the conclusion of each teacher training session before participants leave	All participants in a training session	The training session leaders will administer and collect the questionnaires.
Archive review of financial records*	Throughout the school year at the District Office	All appropriate financial records	The evaluation team will perform the review with the help of the district's business manager.
Interviews with principals and program developers*	The last two weeks of May in principals' and developers' offices	All principals in the district and the program's director and assistant director	The evaluation team will conduct the interviews.

*These instruments will be developed by the evaluation team.

CHAPTER 5

COLLECTING EVALUATION INFORMATION

Collecting evaluation information is a complex task that has a direct bearing on the quality of an evaluation's findings. Among the major information collection activities are validating the information collection instruments and procedures; hiring and training information collectors; implementing the information collection plan; and organizing evaluation information for analysis.

VALIDATING THE INFORMATION COLLECTION INSTRUMENTS AND PROCEDURES

Before information collection for the evaluation begins, the instruments and procedures should be validated through pilot testing and possibly by expert review. The purpose of a pilot test is to answer questions like these:

Will the instruments provide the intended information? Are certain words or questions used in the instruments redundant or misleading? Are the instruments appropriate for their audience?

Can information collectors use the instruments properly? Can they administer, collect, and report information using the written directions and special coding forms?

Are the procedures standardized? Is everyone collecting the information in the same way?

How consistent is the information obtained by the instruments (reliability)?

How accurate is the information obtained with the instruments (validity)?

Pilot testing should be conducted under conditions similar to those expected for the evaluation and should include a representative sample of the evaluation's participants.

The nature and scope of a pilot test can vary considerably. In some cases, very formal pilot tests are required, and pilot test sites are prearranged by the program's or evaluation's sponsors. When no pilot tests are stipulated, it is usually the evaluator's responsibility to find a site and test the information collection procedures. Although a complete pilot test is not always possible, the evaluator should be as thorough as possible within the constraints imposed by time and money. Whenever possible, the same sampling plan proposed for the evaluation should be used to select a minisample for the pilot test. Remember that the individuals who participate in the pilot test should not be included in any subsequent evaluation activities since they will be familiar with the evaluation measures (a threat to the evaluation design's internal validity).

No matter how complete a pilot test might be, there is always the chance that it won't expose all the problems associated with information collection. Therefore, it is helpful to have some experts review the Information Collection Plan, the instruments, and any guides. These experts should have experience and familiarity with the program and its subject area, psychometric skills, and information collection expertise that can be used to help identify and solve potential problems.

Based on the results of the pilot test, information collection instruments and procedures may need to be revised. Depending on the extent of these revisions, pilot testing should be repeated until the evaluator is confident that the information collection activities are feasible and produce credible information.

A Note on Reliability and Validity

Reliability and validity are two concepts used to describe an information collection instrument's technical properties. An instrument is reliable if it provides consistent measurements, and it is valid if it provides accurate and relevant information.

Reliability

A ruler is considered to be a reliable instrument if it yields the same result each time it is used to measure the same object's length—assuming the object itself has not changed. Similarly, an attitude questionnaire would be considered reliable if the results are consistent each time the same person completes it—again assuming the person has not changed. People, of course, are susceptible to change. One day they are more tired, angry, and tense than the next. People also change because of new experiences, or learning, but meaningful changes are not subject to daily fluctuations. A reliable instrument will provide consistent measures of important characteristics despite background fluctuations. Thus, a reliable instrument that measures attitudes is one that provides relatively similar scores from one time to the next as long as an individual's attitude hasn't changed.

Reliability is usually computed by administering an instrument to the same group of persons on two different occasions and then correlating the scores from one time to the next. This procedure is known as "test-retest" reliability. An instrument is considered reliable if the correlation between scores is high, that is, people who score high (or low) on the first occasion also score high (or low) on the second occasion.

Another measure of reliability is how well all the questions on an instrument assess the same skill, characteristic, or quality. This type of reliability is called "homogeneity" or "equivalence." It is computed by dividing an instrument into two equal parts and correlating the scores on one half with the scores on the other half. This procedure is called "split-half" reliability, and it estimates whether both halves of the instrument measure the same skills and characteristics. Another procedure for estimating an instrument's homogeneity is the "Kuder-Richardson Formula 20," also called "coefficient α." This formula is really the average score obtained from computing all possible split-half reliabilities.

Validity

A ruler is considered to be a valid instrument if it provides an accurate measure of a person's height. Similarly, a typing test is considered valid if it provides an accurate measure of an individual's typing ability. To be valid, an instrument must be reliable, and it must actually measure what it is intended to measure. There are four types of validity.

Predictive validity. An instrument can be validated by proving that it predicts an individual's ability to perform a given task. For example, a college entrance examination has predictive validity if it accurately forecasts performance in college. One way of establishing predictive validity is to administer the instrument to all students upon entering college, and then to compare scores on the instrument with their performance in college. If the two sets of scores show a high correlation, the instrument has predictive validity.

Concurrent validity. An instrument can be validated by comparing it against a known measure. A new test of a physician's knowledge, for example, can be compared to an older and valid test to establish concurrent validity, or it can be compared to experts' judgments. If individuals' scores on the new test show high correlation with scores on the older test or with experts' judgments, the new instrument is considered to have concurrent validity.

Content validity. An instrument can be validated by proving that its items or questions are representative of the skills or characteristics that it is intended to measure. For example, a test of seventh-grade vocabulary has content validity if it contains a reasonable sample of words commonly used by seventh graders. Content validity is most frequently established by relying upon experts to determine if the items are a representative sample of the skills and traits that comprise the area to be measured.

Construct validity. An instrument can be validated by demonstrating that it measures a psychological construct like hostility or satisfaction. Construct validity is established experimentally by administering the instrument to persons who are considered by experts to exhibit, in varying degrees, the behaviors associated with the construct. If people who manifest high degrees of the construct also obtain high scores on the instrument, the instrument is considered to have construct validity.

HIRING AND TRAINING INFORMATION COLLECTORS

A completed Information Collection Plan specifies the types of people who will supervise and perform information collection, but it may not actually name each information collector. The ICP may indicate, for example, that the evaluation team will be responsible for mailing questionnaires to the program's participants, but it may not list the individuals who will take specific responsibility for obtaining questionnaire forms, envelopes and stamps, and then monitoring the mailing. Before the evaluation's information collection activities can begin, the evaluator must select the information collection staff.

Members of the evaluation staff, professional data collection agencies, or lay people can be selected to collect information. A major advantage of relying upon the evaluation staff is the control the evaluator exercises over information collection. Another advantage is that direct participation may improve the evaluator's understanding of the program's dynamics and impact. One disadvantage of relying exclusively on the evaluation staff is that information collection usually takes a great deal of time, and may be an inefficient use of resources and of the evaluation staff during peak information collection periods. For instance, a three-person evaluation team based in New York would find it too expensive and physically exhausting to personally administer questionnaires in 20 cities within a three week period of time. Fortunately, professional data collection agencies are available to assist the evaluator, although the skills of their staff are variable and usually not subject to the evaluator's instruction. Sometimes people with no special organizational affiliation (like the residents of a community in which a program is being tried out) can be hired to collect evaluation information as needed. They are a relatively inexpensive source of information collection aid, but they may have no particular commitment to or interest in the evaluation and they may have little or no experience with information collection.

The best way to find professional information collection organizations is to look in the classified sections of professional journals. Personal referrals are also helpful. The best sources for finding and hiring information collectors with no formal organizational affiliation are the faculty and student body of high schools, colleges and universities, employment and social action agencies, personal referrals, previous contacts, and advertisements.

A set of actual criteria given to employment agencies to be used as a guide for finding and hiring information collectors for an evaluation of a health education program is given in the following example.

EXAMPLE: CRITERIA FOR SELECTING INFORMATION COLLECTORS

Preference for the job of field evaluator should be given to individuals:

with a current and valid driver's license

with at least a BA or BS degree

with credits in education, nursing, public health, or public welfare

with experience in the public school system

with sound and practical judgment

with interpersonal skills

who could and would follow directions

who would dress and comport themselves in a way consistent with the expectations of regular school personnel

who would work typical school hours (work beginning at or before 8:00 a.m.)

In selecting the information collection staff be sure to consider these factors:

Availability—Select people who can be present when they are needed to conduct information collection activities. Sometimes the evaluator must work with employers to establish availability. For example, a high school principal may decide that only certain teachers will be able to collect information because other school activities have priority over the evaluation. Sometimes staff schedules determine availability. Nurses on night duty are unlikely to be available to conduct noon interviews, for instance.

Special hiring requirements—Many evaluations are funded by local, state, or federal agencies, all of which are subject to civil rights and equal opportunity legislation, and these laws can affect who can be hired and the speed with which hiring can take place. Affirmative action, for example, requires a waiting period during which any interested individual can apply for the available position.

Bias—The personalities, styles, and attitudes of the information collectors can have a substantial impact on the amount, quality, and accuracy of the information collected. For example, local community members might be able to obtain more candid and valid information from inner city residents than college professors who might be seen as "outsiders."

An important issue closely related to hiring the information collectors is the training they will receive, if any. Because most individuals won't have the ability to communicate with those affected by the program and the technical skills needed in information collection, training is usually necessary.

All training programs for information collectors should have several common themes. Trainees should learn something about the program, the evaluation questions, and the specific information collection activity they will conduct. In addition, they should receive detailed instructions about how to obtain, record and communicate information. To do this, trainees should have a chance to:

- review the information collection instruments
- practice administering the instruments
- practice recording the resulting information
- learn how to report information to the evaluator
- learn how to deal with potential problems

It is also very helpful for trainees to have a "Guide" to information collection in the form of a packet containing copies of all instruments and forms, directions for administering and collecting information, names of people to be contacted and the places to be visited during information collection, names of members of the evaluation staff to be contacted in case of difficulties, and a list of possible problems and solutions. The following example is part of the problem/solution list given to information collectors for an evaluation of a health education program.

EXAMPLE: PROBLEM/SOLUTION LIST FOR INFORMATION COLLECTORS

Problem: You cannot collect the appropriate number of questionnaires because some teachers and nurses have not completed them.
Solution: Try to convince the school of the importance of obtaining the information on as many children as possible. Point out that the Legislature will be making funding decisions on the basis of what you find. If the school is willing, have the staff mail you the forms. If necessary, provide them with a label for the manila envelopes.

IMPLEMENTING THE INFORMATION COLLECTION PLAN
Obtaining clearance

Most information collection activities are subject to legal restrictions. These include limitations on who is eligible to obtain information and the kinds of information that may be collected. As a result, the information collection instruments and procedures usually must receive "clearance." For example, the Office of Management and Budget (OMB) is responsible for clearing information collection activities used in federally-sponsored evaluations. When confronted with clearance requirements, it is a good idea for the evaluator to ask the program monitor or the evaluation's sponsor for assistance. Generally, the steps involved in obtaining clearance are spelled out in complicated directives. Because the intervals between submission of drafts may take many months, the evaluator must organize the information collection schedule to permit enough time for obtaining the necessary authorizations.

Information collection involves many people, and it is the evaluator's responsibility to explain the purpose, nature and schedule of their participation. To do this, the evaluator can hold a meeting or workshop or rely on the mail or telephone. A written description of the program as well as the evaluation and its information collection activities should also be available. Finally, don't forget to thank participants and tell them of the effects of their participation.

Information collection must be carefully monitored to see that it is going according to plan and that all relevant data are being collected and returned. This can be done in several ways. One person on the evaluation staff can take the responsibility for monitoring activities, or two persons can collect identical information independently and the results can be compared for reliability.

Check information as it is returned to determine whether it was collected according to plan, and whether there were any unanticipated or unusual findings or violations of confidentiality.

Information collected during an evaluation is frequently returned to the evaluator in a form that cannot be immediately analyzed. Tests may have to be scored or interview responses may need to be coded and tallied. Information is usually collected at different times and it must be coordinated so that a complete set is eventually available. Also, most evaluations involve gathering large amounts of data that can become unmanageable unless a way is found to organize them. Even an evaluation that only requires a two-page, twenty-five item survey questionnaire to be completed by 300 people would generate 600 pieces of paper and 7,500 bits of information. Finally, the ease with which an evaluation's questions can be answered depends upon how successfully the information collected is organized.

Consider an evaluation question that asks if childrens' perceptions of their teachers are related to their academic achievement. If answers to an open-ended interview question that asked students whether their teachers liked them or not were categorized as "sometimes," "yes," "s/he thinks I'm okay," "I don't like him/her," it would be very difficult to answer the question. On the other hand, if children's responses to the same interview question were categorized to conform to a scale like "definitely yes," "probably yes," "not sure," "probably not," "definitely not," then the evaluation question could be more readily answered. For these reasons, and depending upon the size of the information collection effort, organizing information for analysis can become a major activity requiring careful planning and considerable time. Usually it means categorizing free response data, assigning codes when computer analyses are planned, and rostering data.

To organize evaluation information collected from open-ended questions, the responses must be categorized. This may be done by developing categories in advance and then placing responses into the appropriate slots, or by developing the categories afterwards by sifting through the data to identify natural categories. In response to the question, "What parts of your inservice training were most useful?" if 80 out of 300 people mentioned lectures and only two people mentioned films and readings, then "lectures" would probably be considered one distinct category. Films and readings would fall under a second category, perhaps labelled "other." By relying on preset categories, "lectures," "films," and "readings" might each be considered separate and equal parts of the inservice training program.

Coding is the process of assigning a numerical value to each piece of information. Numerical codes are just names for data that are shorter than words and therefore easier to record, store, analyze, and retrieve. Usually codes are only assigned to information that is going to be analyzed by a computer.

It is possible to assign codes to any kind of evaluation information, such as participant's name, sex, educational background, and hospital's name and geographic location. The choice of which number represents a word is arbitrary. Usually, however, consecutive numbers are chosen, and one number (typically the highest) is reserved for "other" or "no data" categories. In addition, part of the coding process often involves identifying the places on a computer card where the codes will be recorded by keypunchers.

Sample coding directions are presented in the following example:

EXAMPLE: SAMPLE CODING DIRECTIONS

Information	Codes	Location
1. Participant's Name	001 to 999 in alphabetical order	Columns 1-3
2. Participant's Sex	1—Male 2—Female 3—No data	Column 4
3. Participant's Educational Background	1—Some high school 2—High school graduate 3—Some college 4—College graduate 5—Professional or graduate training 9—No data	Column 5
5. Pretest Score	Keypunch total score (0-10)	Columns 6-7
5. Posttest Items 1-10	For each multiple choice item, 1—A 2—B 3—C 4—D 9—No data	Columns 8-17
6. Posttest Score	Keypunch total score (0-10)	Columns 18-19

In order to roster information, the evaluator must identify all the different pieces of data that have been collected and then list them for each individual or group. For example, information from a demographic questionnaire survey of participants, pretest and posttest scores, interviews with principals and a review of school financial records might be rostered as follows. Note that the information has been organized at two levels—the participant and the school.

EXAMPLE: ROSTERING EVALUATION INFORMATION: PARTICIPANT LEVEL

Name	Sex	Education	Pretest Total	Item 1	Item 2	Item 3	Item 4	Item 5	Item 6	Item 7	Item 8	Item 9	Item 10	Posttest Total
0 0 1	1	4	0 2	1	2	3	1	4	9	1	4	2	2	0 3
0 0 2	1	2	0 4	9	2	2	2	1	4	3	2	2	9	0 5
0 0 3	1	2	0 5	1	2	2	2	3	2	4	4	4	9	0 4
0 0 4	2	3	0 3	2	2	2	2	2	9	4	3	2	1	0 6
0 0 5	2	9	0 5	1	2	3	4	9	2	2	2	2	2	0 6
0 0 6	1	5	0 4	2	2	2	2	9	1	2	3	3	3	0 5
0 0 7	2	1	0 3	1	3	4	9	1	2	2	2	2	2	0 5
0 0 8	2	9	0 5	2	2	2	3	9	2	9	9	9	2	0 5
0 0 9	2	1	0 5	2	2	2	2	2	1	2	2	2	2	0 9
0 1 0	1	3	0 2	1	1	1	1	3	9	3	1	2	2	0 2

45

EXAMPLE: ROSTERING EVALUATION INFORMATION: SCHOOL LEVEL

School		Principal Interview Items										Per pupil cost				Textbook cost		
		1	2	3	4	5	6	7	8	9	10							
0	1	1	1	2	2	3	3	1	1	2	1	0	8	8	7	0	5	2
0	2	2	6	5	3	3	4	2	4	2	1	0	9	2	8	0	5	5
0	3	3	2	3	4	3	5	2	3	3	2	1	8	1	8	0	4	2
0	4	4	5	4	4	3	5	1	5	1	3	1	7	6	9	1	9	1
0	5	1	3	4	3	3	7	1	5	1	3	1	5	3	6	5	4	6
0	6	2	4	5	1	3	2	2	5	2	1	0	8	8	6	9	4	9
0	7	3	1	2	2	3	1	1	5	3	2	0	9	9	7	3	1	2
0	8	4	6	5	3	3	3	2	4	1	3	1	4	2	8	3	4	8
0	9	1	2	3	4	3	9	1	3	1	3	1	4	4	9	0	0	6
1	0	2	5	4	3	3	4	9	2	3	2	1	7	6	7	4	2	8
1	1	3	3	4	2	3	3	2	1	2	1	1	7	2	7	5	5	6
1	2	4	4	3	2	3	3	1	3	2	1	1	6	5	7	2	2	3
1	3	1	9	1	9	3	1	9	5	3	9	1	4	3	6	3	1	9
1	4	2	1	2	1	3	5	1	5	9	3	0	9	9	9	3	0	2
1	5	3	6	5	2	3	9	2	9	3	2	0	8	7	9	4	1	6
1	6	4	2	1	1	3	9	1	1	2	1	1	4	4	7	5	3	8

CHAPTER 6
PLANNING AND CONDUCTING INFORMATION ANALYSIS ACTIVITIES

The evaluator must think about information analysis even before collection of evaluation information begins. The methods actually used for analysis range from statistics-based methods most frequently used by experimental psychologists and sociologists to scholarship-based methods often used by historians and anthropologists. All of these attempt to describe evaluation information by tallies or frequency counts, summaries, averages, and measures of variation and range. They also attempt to explain evaluation information by comparing groups, identifying patterns and trends in events, and establishing relationships among variables.

CHOOSING INFORMATION ANALYSIS METHODS

The evaluation questions frame the entire evaluation, and analysis methods must be chosen so that the questions can be directly answered. The design strategy and information collection plan also must be coordinated with one another and with the information analyses. If the evaluation uses a true experimental design, for example, then objective information collection activities and statistical analyses would be required. The evaluator's training and experience may also influence preference for and comfort with particular analysis methods. No matter what background the evaluator has, however, the choice must be guided by the technical appropriateness of the analysis method. All analysis procedures have underlying assumptions which, if not met, can invalidate analysis findings. Finally, the entire evaluation depends upon available resources. Some analytic methods are more expensive than others because they depend on special equipment like computers.

Frequently Used Analysis Methods

Analysis methods that are frequently used by evaluators are:
- Descriptive statistics
- Correlation statistics
- Regression
- Univariate analysis of variance
- Analysis of covariance
- Multivariate analysis of variance
- Chi square

Descriptive Statistics

Descriptive statistics describe data in terms of measures of central tendency (e.g., mode, median, mean), variability (e.g., standard deviation and range), and frequency (e.g., the number of responses to each alternative in multiple-choice questions; the number of persons getting a total score of 62, 75, 100). They can be used to answer evaluation questions like these:

- Did the number of students performing at grade level increase?
- Did a majority of the participants agree that the program met their needs?
- How similar were attitudes about national health insurance at the end of the program?

Descriptive statistics are among the most useful analysis techniques in evaluations because they are inherently meaningful and easily understood. They are the units for more complex and less intuitive statistical procedures. The following example illustrates how descriptive statistics can be used to analyze evaluation information.

EXAMPLE: SIMPLE DESCRIPTIVE STATISTICS

Program Description: **The goal of the program is to teach college students interpersonal communication skills. To accomplish this goal, students view videotaped conversations between two persons and are trained to distinguish between what speakers say and what they mean by observing content, tone, context, and body language. The program is judged to be successful if students learn to adequately use content, tone, context, and body language to interpret conversations.**

Evaluation Question: **Are students able to use content, tone, context, and body language to interpret conversations?**

Design Strategy; **A case design was used in which all students who enrolled in selected undergraduate communication courses participated in the interpersonal communication skills program during three weeks of the fall semester. The dependent variable was an ability to interpret conversations as measured by an achievement test. The independent variable was studied at only one level: participation in the interpersonal communication skills program.**

Information Collection Plan: **A test was given to all participating students at the end of the course. The highest possible score on the test was 100 points, with adequate performance defined as a score of 70 or better.**

Analysis Plan: **Descriptive statistics were computed from students' total test scores at the end of the three-week program.**

Analysis Results:

$\overline{X}$	SD	N	Range	Number of Students Who Achieved a Score of 70 or Better
78.8	13.6	130	44-96	71

Interpretation: **One hundred and thirty students (N=130) completed the program. Their average score ($\overline{X}$) was 78.8 points, which is above the criterion, and 71 students demonstrated an adequate ability to interpret conversation. The relatively small standard deviation (SD) and range indicate that each student's ability is similar to the others.**

Correlations measure the relationship between two variables, a dependent variable and an independent variable (e.g., numbers of years of schooling and salary) and are reported within a range of +1 (perfect positive correlation) to −1 (perfect negative correlation). When high values on one variable occur simultaneously with high values on another, the two variables are said to be positively correlated, and when high values on one variable occur with low values on another, the two variables are said to be negatively correlated. Correlations can be used to answer evaluation questions like:

- What is the relationship between self concept and number of visits to the school nurse?
- Can scores on college entrance examinations be used to identify people who are likely to succeed in the new management training program?
- Is vocational preference correlated with parents' job experiences?

Correlations are used to identify relationships between variables, but they cannot be used to establish causation. For instance, a correlation analysis can show that people who have completed many years of schooling usually earn high salaries, but it cannot show that people earn high salaries *because* they had many years of schooling.

The following example illustrates how correlation statistics can be used to analyze evaluation information.

EXAMPLE: CORRELATION STATISTICS

Program Description: The goal of the program is to improve fourth-grade students' reading ability. Teachers for the program have been selected because they have at least three years of teaching experience and have master's degrees in reading education. The program takes place throughout the school year and occupies one hour a day of each student's time. The program is considered successful if, at the end of the year, students' reading levels are above the national norm.

Evaluation Background: Preliminary evaluation findings indicated that some students did very well with the program, while others did badly, and the evaluator was asked to identify factors that distinguished among them. One of the factors studied was birth order.

Evaluation question: Is there a relationship between birth order and success in the program? (Birth order refers to whether a child is the first-born, second-born, etc.)

Design Strategy: A case design was used for the evaluation, and it included all students who participated in the program. The dependent variable was success in the program as measured by students' scores on an achievement test. The independent variable was students' birth order.

Information Collection Plan: A 500-point, nationally-normed achievement test was given to all participating fourth-grade students at the end of the school year. Students' birth orders were determined from school records.

Analysis Plan: Students' raw scores on the reading achievement test and their birth orders were correlated, using the Pearson Product Moment Formula.

Analysis Results: A correlation coefficient (r) of –0.89 was obtained based on data from 206 students.

$$N = 206$$
$$r = -.89$$
$$r^2 = .79$$

Interpretation: A high negative correlation (r= –.89) was found between students' reading scores and their birth orders, indicating that 79% ($r^2 = .79$) of the total variation in students' reading scores could be accounted for by their position of birth. This finding suggests that first-and second-born students are more successful with the program (have higher reading scores) than the others. (It cannot be concluded that first-and second-born students are necessarily smarter.)

Regression

Regression is a method for examining the relationship between a dependent variable and two or more independent variables. If there is only one independent variable, then regression is equivalent to correlation statistics. Regression can be used to predict the value of a dependent variable based on values of one or more independent variables. Regression analysis can also be used to answer a question like, "What is the relationship between students' mathematics performance (the dependent variable) and the number of hours of instruction received, grade level, and sex (the three independent variables)?" The use of regression analysis in answering this question can be expressed mathematically as an equation of the form:

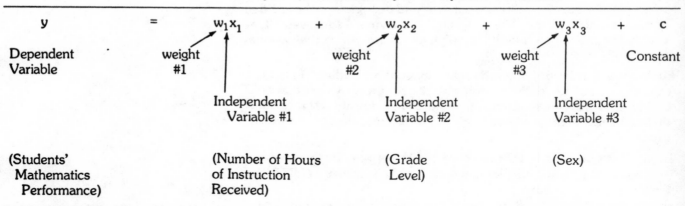

This equation shows the relationship between a dependent variable (y) and three independent variables (x_1, x_2, x_3). The weights (w_1, w_2, w_3) or regression coefficients are computed as part of the analysis and reflect the contribution of each independent variable in explaining the dependent variable. That is, if w_1 is greater than w_2 and w_3, then x_1 is the independent variable that contributes most to an understanding of y, the dependent variable. (For such interpretations to be made, x_1, x_2, and x_3 must be measured using the same metric, or alternately, w_1, w_2, and w_3 must be normalized or standardized as part of the computations for the regression analysis.)

The following example illustrates how regression analysis might be used in an evaluation study.

EXAMPLE: REGRESSION

Program Description: The purpose of the program is to provide asthmatic children with the skills needed to care for themselves whenever possible. Major activities include having specially trained nurses teach asthmatic children and their parents to perform special breathing exercises, to remain calm during attacks, to recognize the early warning signs of attacks, how to treat them, and when to seek medical assistance. The nurses decide how many hours children should be counseled. Fewer absences from school because of asthma attacks is considered evidence of the program's merit.

Evaluation Background: Preliminary evaluation data showed that some children only received five hours of counseling, whereas others received as many as 25 hours, with an average of ten hours per child. Since the major cost of the program was the salaries of the specially trained nurse counselors, the evaluator was asked to investigate the relationship between benefit from the program and the number of hours children are counseled, taking into account their age and the severity of their asthma.

Evaluation Question: What is the relationship between number of absences from school and hours of counseling, severity of asthma at the beginning of the program, and age?

Design Strategy: A case design was used for the evaluation. The dependent variable was the number of days a child was absent from school because of asthma attacks. The independent variables were (1) the number of hours of counseling a child received, (2) the severity of a child's asthma at the beginning of the program, and (3) a child's age. All school-age children who were being treated by a physician at the SunDay Clinic and who began their counseling program between September and November were included in the evaluation.

Information Collection Plan: School records were reviewed to obtain information about a child's age and the number of asthma-related school absences each child had for a six-month period, beginning with the first day of counseling. Physicians were asked to rate the severity of their patients' asthma on a nine-point scale, with 1 as "extremely mild" and 9 as "extremely severe." Counselors were asked to keep records of how many hours they spent counseling each child.

Analysis Plan: A multiple-regression analysis was conducted. The weights for each independent variable were transformed as part of the analysis so that they were reported in terms of the same ten-point scale in the regression equation.

Analysis Results: The results of the regression analysis were:

Regression Results

$$y = 501x_1 - 2.11x_2 + 0.07x_3 + 25.01$$

Number of Absences $\quad$ Severity $\quad$ Hours in Counseling $\quad$ Age

$R^2 = .85$

The regression equation shows that the severity of a child's asthma was the independent variable with the highest degree of relationship to number of absences. Hours in counseling was also important and bore a negative relationship to number of absences; that is, higher numbers of absences were associated with fewer hours of counseling. Age made a negligible contribution to the equation. The explanatory capability (R^2) of the regression equation was high, with 85% of the total variation in the dependent variable being accounted for by the three independent variables.

Interpretation: The results of a multiple-regression analysis demonstrated a relationship between number of absences from school and severity of a child's asthma, number of hours of counseling received, and age. In particular, the more severe a child's asthma, the greater the number of absences from school. With more hours of counseling, however, fewer absences can be expected. Furthermore, a child's age does not affect this pattern. These findings suggest that if a child got more counseling, the number of school absences could be reduced. For example, by increasing counseling hours from ten to fifteen, the expected number of absences could be decreased from 14.63 to 4.08 days for a ten-year-old child with a severity rating of 2 and from 44.69 to 34.14 days for a ten-year-old child with a severity rating of 8, a reduction of 10.55 days in both cases.

Analysis of Variance (ANOVA)

ANOVA is a collection of statistical procedures for comparing the average performance of two or more groups or for studying groups' average performance over time. ANOVA is used in evaluations to answer questions like:

- Is there a difference between participants in the experimental program and the traditional program in their attitude toward continuing education?
- Did the experimental program participants' attitude toward continuing education change from the beginning to the middle to the end of the year?
- Do males and females who participate in the experimental and the traditional programs have different attitudes toward continuing education?

In ANOVA, only one dependent variable can be analyzed at a time, although there may be several independent variables. If there is just one independent variable, the analysis is called a one-way ANOVA; if there are two independent variables, it is called a two-way ANOVA, and so on.*

To make comparisons with ANOVA, it is necessary to restate the evaluation questions as propositions or hypotheses to be accepted or rejected. For example, the first evaluation question could be rephrased as a hypothesis in one of two ways:

Hypothesis 1: On the average, the attitudes toward continuing education of participants in the experimental program and the traditional program are equal.

Hypothesis 2: On the average, the attitudes toward continuing education

---

*Another way of describing ANOVAs is based on the number of levels at which each independent variable is being studied, as well as the number of independent variables included in the analysis. For example, an ANOVA that involves three independent variables each being studied at two levels would be called a 2x2x2 ANOVA, using this scheme, rather than a three-way ANOVA.

of participants in the experimental program and the traditional program are different.

Because of its mathematical structure, ANOVA cannot prove directly that there are differences between groups. It can only prove that the opposite (that there are no differences or that the groups are the same) is not true. Thus, ANOVA tests hypotheses about the sameness or equality of behavior and not the differences, and for the first evaluation question, ANOVA would test Hypothesis #1. This hypothesis is often called the null hypothesis.

The second evaluation question, concerning possible changes in attitude, might be answered with a one-way ANOVA. The analysis would involve one dependent variable, attitude towards continuing education, and one independent variable, time, to be studied at three levels: the beginning, the middle, and the end of the program. The null hypothesis that the ANOVA would test is that participants' average attitudes towards continuing education at the beginning, middle, and end of the program are equal. This hypothesis can be expressed as:

Ho: $\overline{X}_1 = \overline{X}_2 = \overline{X}_3$ where $\overline{X}_i$ = average attitude at time i (i = 1, 2, 3)

Hypotheses associated with an ANOVA are tested with an F-statistic, which is derived mathematically by dividing the total variation in the dependent variable into components and then comparing different estimates of the variance components with one another. If the estimates are similar, then the value of the F-statistic will be a small number, and the hypothesis that the average performance of two or more programs is equal cannot be rejected. If the estimates are not similar, then the F-value will be a large number, and the hypothesis can be rejected. Rejecting the hypothesis would mean that the average performance of the programs is not equal, but it would not permit inferences about whether one program's average performance was greater or smaller than another's. When an F-test for an independent variable that is being studied at more than two levels results in rejecting the hypothesis of equality of means, all that is known is that some group's performance is different, and additional analyses (like Newman-Keuls) must be conducted to determine which group's mean performance is significantly higher or lower than the others. For independent variables being studied at only two levels, this is not necessary since rejecting the hypothesis that the means are equal automatically implies that the group with the higher mean score performed statistically significantly better than the other group.

Statistical tables are available that list the smallest value that an F-statistic can take in order to reject a hypothesis. These tables provide F-values for different degrees of freedom (df) and significance levels (p). Degrees of freedom refer to the number of independent scores (or observations) used in computing the statistic. The level of significance refers to the probability of falsely rejecting the hypothesis that the mean performance is equal. Social scientists usually use the .05 or .01 significance level, which means that there are either five chances in 100 or one chance in 100 of falsely rejecting the hypothesis.

When comparing two groups *only*, it is possible to test the hypothesis of the equality of the two groups' means using a t-statistic instead of an F-statistic. If two independent or different groups are being compared, the hypothesis of equality of group means could be tested either by a one-way ANOVA or an independent t-test. If two dependent or the same groups are being compared, either a one-way repeated-measures ANOVA or a dependent t-test will yield the same results.

The following example illustrates how ANOVA might be used to analyze evaluation information.

EXAMPLE: TWO-WAY ANOVA

Program Description: One of the purposes of the new career education program, unlike the traditonal program, is to provide students with a better understanding of the specific jobs available in different career areas. The two programs will be evaluated to find out how much they have influenced students' satisfaction with their career choices.

Evaluation Background: A previous evaluation found that 95% of all the career education students were working in occupations for which they were trained in high school.

Evaluation Questions:

1. Are students who participated in the new program more satisfied with their careers than students who participated in the traditional program?

2. Is there a difference in career satisfaction among students who (in high school) were interested in careers in business, the arts, or the sciences?

3. What is the association between (interaction) the particular career education program in which students participate, students' career interest while in high school, and students' satisfaction with their careers?

Design Strategy: A comparison group design strategy was used for the evaluation. There were two independent variables, program participation (which was studied at two levels: the new and the traditional programs) and career interest (which was studied at three levels: business, the arts, and the sciences). The dependent variable was career satisfaction.

Ninety-six twelfth-grade students at Lincoln High School participated in the evaluation. A random stratified sampling plan was used to assign them to groups. First, 32 students from all those students interested in business, 32 students from all those interested in the arts, and 32 from all those interested in the sciences were selected using a table of random numbers. Then, using the same table, from each set of 32 students, 16 were assigned to the traditional program and the remaining 16 to the new program.

Career Interests	Program:		Total
	New	Traditional	
Business	16	16	32
The Arts	16	16	32
The Sciences	16	16	32
Total	48	48	96

Information Collection Plan: Five years after they were graduated from high school, all participants in the evaluation were sent a questionnaire in the mail. The questionnaire was designed to measure career satisfaction, and responses were reported on a scale of 1 (low) to 75 (high).

Analysis Method: The first step of the analysis process was to compute descriptive statistics. Based on a review of the descriptive statistics, there appeared to be sufficient differences in mean scores to warrant an ANOVA. In the second step of the analysis, a two-way ANOVA was performed that tested three hypothesis:

Hypothesis 1 (H_1): The average career satisfaction of students in the new and traditional program is equal.

$$H_1 : \overline{P}_1 = \overline{P}_2$$

$\overline{P}_1 =$ Average student satisfaction for students in the new program

$\overline{P}_2 =$ Average student satisfaction for students in the traditional program

Hypothesis 2 (H_2): The average career satisfaction of students whose career interests in high school were in business, the arts, and the sciences is equal.

$$H_2 : \overline{I}_1 = \overline{I}_2 = \overline{I}_3$$

$\overline{I}_1 =$ Average satisfaction of students interested in business

$\overline{I}_2 =$ Average satisfaction of students interested in the arts

$\overline{I}_3 =$ Average satisfaction of students interested in the sciences

Hypothesis 3 (H_3): The average career satisfaction of students in each of the six program/high school interest groups is equal.

$$H_3 : \overline{P_1 I_1} = \overline{P_1 I_2} = \overline{P_1 I_3} = \overline{P_2 I_1} = \overline{P_2 I_2} = \overline{P_2 I_3}$$

where $\overline{P_1 I_1} =$ Average satisfaction of students in the new program whose high school career interest was in business

The third step of the analysis involved the use of the Newman-Keuls procedure to determine where differences existed. This step was taken whenever an F-test resulted in rejecting the hypothesis about equality of means.

Analysis results:

Descriptive Statistics

	New Program	Traditional Program
Business	$\overline{X} = 46.36$ SD = 3.46 N = 16	$\overline{X} = 45.33$ SD = 3.78 N = 16
The Arts	$\overline{X} = 49.39$ SD = 4.02 N = 16	$\overline{X} = 49.36$ SD = 4.47 N = 16
The Sciences	$\overline{X} = 53.48$ SD = 4.02 N = 16	$\overline{X} = 50.22$ SD = 4.52 N = 16

ANOVA Table

Source of Variation	Degrees of Freedom	Mean Squares	F-value	Signifi-cance (p)
Programs (H_1)	1	49.59	3.22	ns
Career Interests (H_2)	2	291.33	18.94	< .01
Programs x Career Interest Interaction (H_3)	2	21.82	1.42	ns
Error	90	15.38		

The test of the first hypothesis (H_1) resulted in an F-value of 3.22, which is not statistically significant. Consequently, the hypothesis that the mean career satisfaction of participants in the new and traditional programs is equal cannot be rejected.

The test of the second hypothesis (H_2) resulted in an F-value of 18.94, which is statistically significant at the .01 level, indicating that there is a difference in career satisfaction among students whose high school career interests were in business, the arts and the sciences. Further analysis, using the Newman-Keuls procedure, showed that students with business interests had significantly lower career satisfaction than students interested in the arts or the sciences, but that there were no differences between students interested in the arts or the sciences in terms of their career satisfaction.

The test of the third hypothesis (H_3) resulted in an F-value of 1.42, which is not statistically significant. Consequently, the hypothesis that there is an interaction between program participation and high school career interests cannot be rejected. This result can be seen in the following figure in which the almost parallel nature of the lines indicates little or no interaction.

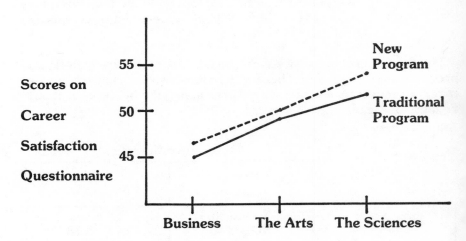

High School Career Interests

Interpretation: A two-way ANOVA was conducted to answer Evaluation Questions 1, 2, and 3. The analysis was unable to uncover differences in mean career satisfaction between participants in the new and traditional programs. This suggests that students who participated in the new program were not more satisfied with their careers than students in the traditional program (Evaluation Question 1).

The ANOVA did, however, reveal statistically significant differences in career satisfaction among students whose high school career interests were in business, the arts, and the sciences. Further analysis (using the Newman-Keuls procedure) revealed that the career satisfaction of students with business interests was statistically significantly lower than that of students with interests in the arts and sciences, but that there were no significant differences in career satisfaction between students with interests in the arts and sciences (Evaluation Question 2).

The ANOVA was unable to confirm a statistically significant relationship between type of program and high school career interests. This suggests that there is no interaction between type of program and career interests in terms of students' career satisfaction (Evaluation Question 3).

Analysis of Covariance (ANCOVA)

ANCOVA is a form of ANOVA in which the dependent variable is "corrected" by adjusting for the effects of an outside variable called a covariate. Consider an evaluation question that asks if one of two speech therapy programs is more successful in correcting stuttering. If participants in one program are older than those in the other and it is suggested in the literature that there is a relationship between age and success in speech therapy programs, then using ANOVA to compare the groups' performance at the end of their programs would be unfair since one group (the younger) probably began with a handicap. However, ANCOVA could be used to adjust the end-of-program performance scores to take into account age differences. For this analysis, the dependent variable would be end of program speech performance, the covariate would be age, and the independent variable would be program participation (which is being studied at two levels: Program 1 and Program 2).

Mathematically, the correction to the dependent variable is derived with the following regression equation:

$$\underset{\text{variable}}{\underset{\text{dependent}}{y}} = \underset{\underset{\text{covariate}}{\text{weight}\uparrow}}{wx} + \underset{\text{constant}}{c}$$

The corrected dependent variable is obtained by subtracting the value of the dependent variable computed using the regression equation from its actual (observed) value:

$$\underset{\text{corrected}}{y} = \underset{\text{actual}}{y} - \underset{\text{regression}}{y}$$

where:

y corrected = the adjusted end-of-program speech performance score corrected to take account of differences related to participants' age.

y actual = the observed value of the end-of-program speech performance level.

y regression = the predicted speech performance score based on knowledge of participants' age and computed from the regression equation.

The types of evaluation questions that can be answered with ANCOVA are similar to those that can be answered with ANOVA. In addition, the hypotheses tested with ANCOVA about the equality of group means are analogous to those tested with ANOVA, except that in ANCOVA, mean performance scores are corrected for the effects of the covariate. For example, for the evaluation of the two speech therapy programs, ANCOVA could be used to test the hypothesis that the end-of-program speech performance scores corrected for age differences among participants were equal.

Many strict requirements circumscribe the use of ANCOVA. One of them is that the covariate be measured before the program takes place. Another is that the regression equations relating the dependent variable to the covariate for each program group be parallel. These requirements can be difficult to meet, but without them, ANCOVA is not valid. The following example illustrates how ANCOVA might be used for an evaluation.

EXAMPLE: ANCOVA

Program Description: The State commissioned an evaluation to compare three of its energy conservation programs to determine if any of them results in significant savings of natural gas.

Evaluation Question: Is there a difference in the amount of natural gas consumed by participants in Program 1, Program 2, and Program 3?

Design Strategy: A comparison group evaluation design strategy was used. The independent variable was program (which was studied at three levels: Programs 1, 2, and 3) and the dependent variable was level of consumption of natural gas. Seventy-five elementary schools were selected at random to participate in each of the three programs.

Information Collection Plan: Gas company records were reviewed to determine how many cubic feet of natural gas were consumed by each school during the three-month period immediately before the programs began and one year after they were in operation.

Analysis Method: The first step of the analysis process was to compare, using ANOVA, the gas consumption of schools assigned to each group immediately before the programs began. The results showed that the program groups were significantly different from one another. The requirements for ANCOVA were then tested, and the data were found to be appropriate. Consequently, during the second step of the analysis, an ANCOVA was performed to compare the three groups' gas consumption at the end of one year of program operation, taking into account initial preprogram differences. The ANCOVA tested the hypothesis that the three groups' adjusted average gas consumption was equal.

Analysis Results:

ANCOVA Table

Source of Variation	Degrees of Freedom	Mean Squares	F-value	Significance
Programs	2	0.598	2.29	ns
Error (within groups)	221	0.261		

58

The ANCOVA resulted in an F-value of 2.29, which is not statistically significant. Therefore, the hypothesis that at the end of one year of operation, the three program groups' average gas consumption corrected for initial differences was equal could not be rejected.

Interpretation: The ANCOVA was unable to uncover statistically significant differences in average gas consumption among the schools participating in each of the state's three experimental energy conservation programs.

Multivariate Analysis of Variance (MANOVA)

MANOVA is analogous to ANOVA, except that more than one dependent variable is considered. For example, an experimental and a control group might be compared in terms of a combination of attitude and achievement scores. MANOVA can be used to answer evaluation questions like these:

- From the beginning to the end of the program, did participants' attendance and performance improve?
- How does Program A compare with Program B in terms of the cost per participant and the staff's satisfaction with their jobs?

The purpose of MANOVA, like ANOVA, is to determine whether statistically significant differences exist between two or more groups, but in MANOVA these differences are based upon the group members' scores on a set of dependent variables, rather than on a single dependent variable as in ANOVA. Similarly, MANOVA, like ANOVA, involves testing hypotheses about the equality of group means; in MANOVA, however, the means are really a set of averages, one for each dependent variable. Mathematically, the multivariate mean is represented by a vector whose elements are a group's mean scores on each dependent variable.

Multivariate analysis of variance is used in an evaluation when the behavior of importance is defined in terms of several dependent variables that are believed or known to be interrelated. Suppose two programs are being compared to find which is best for reducing the number of school absences and for improving citizenship grades, and that instructional theory or experience has shown these variables to be related, then MANOVA is an appropriate analysis method. An alternative would be to compute two separate ANOVAs, but this second method is not preferred since there is an increased probability of chance errors. Each time a statistical test is performed, there is a probability of making an error of falsely rejecting the hypothesis, and this probability increases as the number of tests increases. Consequently, it is more efficient to compute one MANOVA involving several dependent variables than to compute a separate ANOVA for each dependent variable.

For each hypothesis that is tested, the first step in a MANOVA is to test the equality of means using a multivariate F-value. If the F-value is significant, then the hypothesis can be rejected and additional analyses might be conducted to determine if there are significant differences when the dependent variables are considered separately. One method of doing this is to conduct step-down F-tests in which ANOVAs are performed on single dependent variables that have been adjusted to remove the effects of the other dependent variables. For example, if a multivariate F-test results in rejecting the hypothesis that the experimental and control groups' performances are equal in terms of number of absences and citizenship grades (considered as a unit), then step-down F-tests might be conducted to determine if there are statistically significant citizenship differences between the groups and whether there are significant differences in absences between the groups, removing the effects of citizenship. On the other hand, if the multivariate F-test is not significant, then no additional analyses need be conducted. An example that illustrates how MANOVA might be used for an evaluation follows.

EXAMPLE:MULTIVARIATE ANALYSIS OF VARIANCE (MANOVA)

Program: The state government has commissioned an evaluation of its bilingual-bicultural education programs. These programs can be distinguished from one another by the type of curriculum materials used and by teachers' training. Three types of curriculum materials are used: (1) traditional curriculum materials, (2) curriculum materials that emphasize language development, and (3) curriculum materials that focus on experience in using languages. Teachers in the programs have either had a traditional training in elementary education or have participated in the state's special bilingual-bicultural teacher training program.

Evaluation Questions:

(1) Is there a statistically significant difference among programs using different curriculum materials in terms of students' general school achievement, level of parental involvement, students' reading ability at the conclusion of the program, and teacher performance?

(2) Is there a statistically significant difference among programs having teachers with different training in terms of students' general school achievement, level of parental involvement, students' reading ability at the conclusion of the program, and teacher performance?

(3) Is there an interaction between type of curriculum materials used and teacher training in terms of students' general school achievement, level of parental involvement, students' reading ability at the conclusion of the program, and teacher performance?

Design Strategy: A comparison group design strategy was used for the evaluation. There were two independent variables, curriculum materials (which was studied at three levels: traditional, language development, and language experience), and teacher training (which was studied at two levels: traditional and special). There were four dependent variables: (1) students' general school achievement, (2) level of parental involvement, (3) students' reading ability at the conclusion of the program and (4) teacher performance.

Eight out of the 78 school districts in the state participated in the evaluation. Every district contributed twelve fourth-grade classrooms, two of which were randomly assigned to each of the six possible program groups.

The Sample of Classrooms

Teacher Training \ Curriculum Materials	Traditional	Language Development	Language Experience
Traditional	16	16	16
Special	16	16	16

Information Collection Plan: Information about students' general school achievement was obtained from the nationally normed standardized test which is administered to all students in the district in May. The maximum possible score on this test is 100 points. Students' reading ability at the end of the program was measured with a specially designed 75-question test containing Spanish and English items. Information about parental involvement was collected by reviewing school records, and the data were reported on a 100-point scale (with 100 as the highest possible score). Each teacher was rated by three trained observers on a five-point scale (with 5 as the highest score), and the average of the three ratings was computed to obtain an index of teacher performance.

Analysis Method: Multivariate analysis of variance (MANOVA) was used to test three hypotheses:

Hypothesis 1 (H_1): Taking all four dependent variables into account, the average performance for the classrooms using each type of curriculum materials is equal.

$H_1 : \overline{C}_1 = \overline{C}_2 = \overline{C}_3$, where $\overline{C}_1$ = Traditional

$\overline{C}_2$ = Language development

$\overline{C}_3$ = Language experience

Hypothesis 2 (H_2): Taking all four dependent variables into account, the average performance in classrooms with traditionally and specially trained teachers is equal.

$H_2 : \overline{T}_1 = \overline{T}_2$, where $\overline{T}_1$ = Traditional training

$\overline{T}_2$ = Special training

Hypothesis 3 (H_3): Taking all four dependent variables into account, the average performance in each of the six program groups is equal.

$H_3 : \overline{C}_1\overline{T}_1 = \overline{C}_1\overline{T}_2 = \overline{C}_2\overline{T}_1 = \overline{C}_2\overline{T}_2 = \overline{C}_3\overline{T}_1 = \overline{C}_3\overline{T}_2$

Analysis Results: Results of descriptive statistics demonstrated sufficient differences among group means to warrant further analysis.

Descriptive Statistics

		Traditional Training			*Special Training*		
		Traditional	Language Development	Language Experience	Traditional	Language Development	Language Experience
General School Achievement	X=	86.50	87.51	88.51	85.49	87.52	88.46
	SD=	3.17	3.17	3.22	3.16	3.18	3.07
	N=	16	16	16	16	16	16
Parental Involvement	X=	73.75	73.75	72.91	71.98	78.80	80.00
	SD=	18.26	18.01	17.45	19.11	15.99	19.01
	N=	16	16	16	16	16	16
Reading Ability	X=	45.33	49.36	50.22	46.36	49.40	50.48
	SD=	3.78	4.46	4.52	3.46	3.08	4.02
	N=	16	16	16	16	16	16
Teacher Performance	X=	3.88	4.14	4.20	4.46	4.47	4.42
	SD=	0.47	0.38	0.57	0.60	0.58	0.52
	N=	16	16	16	16	16	16

Because the dependent variables were thought to be interrelated, each of them was correlated with the others. The generally high correlation coefficients that resulted justified the use of MANOVA.

Correlation Table

	General School Achievement	Level of Parental Involvement	Reading Ability	Teacher Performance
General School Achievement	1.000			
Level of Parental Involvement	-0.833	1.000		
Reading Ability	0.294	-0.250	1.000	
Teacher Performance	0.173	-0.137	0.373	1.000

The MANOVA for the first hypothesis (H_1) resulted in a multivariate F-value of 0.728, with eight and 174 degrees of freedom, which was not statistically significant. Consequently, the hypothesis that the average performance in classrooms using each of three types of curriculum materials is equal could not be rejected.

The MANOVA for the second hypothesis (H_2) resulted in a multivariate F-value of 3.214 with four and 87 degrees of freedom, which was significant at the 0.05 level. Consequently, the hypothesis that the average performance in classrooms with traditionally and specially trained teachers is equal, taking all four dependent variables into account, was rejected. Because the multivariate test was significant, a series of step-down F-values were then computed.

Step-Down F-Test Results

Dependent Variable	Step-Down F-value	Significance (p)
General School Achievement	4.72	< .01
Reading Ability	3.95	< .01
Parental Involvement	1.01	ns
Teacher Performance	0.08	ns

The results of the first test ($F = 4.72$, $p < .01$) showed that there were statistically significant differences between classrooms with specially and traditionally trained teachers in terms of students' general school achievement. Classrooms with specially trained teachers had higher levels of general school achievement than classrooms with traditionally trained teachers. The results of the second step-down test ($F = 3.95$, $p < .01$) showed that there were also statistically significant differences between classrooms in terms of students' reading ability at the conclusion of the program, even when the effects of general school achievement were removed. The reading of students in classrooms having specially trained teachers was significantly higher than for students in classrooms with traditionally trained teachers. The results of the third test ($F = 1.01$, p = ns) indicated that there were no statistically significant differences between classrooms with respect to parental involvement when the effects of general school achievement and reading ability were removed. The results of the fourth test ($F = 0.08$, $p =$ ns) found no significant differences between classrooms in terms of teacher performance when the effects of all other dependent variables were removed.

The MANOVA analysis for the third hypothesis (H_3) resulted in a multivariate F-value of 0.830, with four and 174 degrees of freedom, which was not significant and therefore, the hypothesis that the performance of all six treatment groups is equal could not be rejected.

Interpretation: A multivariate analysis of variance that considered as a unit general school achievement, level of parental involvement, reading ability at the conclusion of the program, and teacher performance, showed that there were no statistically significant differences among classrooms using traditional language development, and language experience curriculum materials (Evaluation Question 1).

The MANOVA did reveal statistically significant differences between programs with specially and traditionally trained teachers. A series of step-down F-tests were conducted to determine if significant differences could be found for each dependent variable. The results showed that the general school achievement of students whose teachers were specially trained was significantly higher than students whose teachers were traditionally trained. It was also found that in classrooms with specially trained teachers, students' reading ability at the conclusion of the program was significantly greater, even after the effects of general school achievement were taken into account. Significant differences were found between classrooms with specially trained and traditionally trained teachers in terms of level of parental involvement and teacher performance (Evaluation Question 2).

The MANOVA did not reveal significant interaction between type of curriculum used and teacher training (Evaluation Question 3).

Chi Square

Variables that are expressed in terms of classes that can be distinguished from one another but that cannot be arranged into a hierarchy are said to provide categorical information. For example, classifying sex as male or female and program satisfaction as high or low will produce categorical data. The chi square statistic is used to analyze categorical information. Two procedures that are frequently required for evaluations and that employ the chi square statistic are goodness-of-fit testing and contingency table analysis.

Goodness of Fit Testing   Goodness-of-fit is a procedure for comparing empirically derived data (expressed as frequencies) with those that can be expected in theory. An evaluation question that could be answered using goodness-of-fit testing is:

How do participants' reactions to the XYZ Program compare with experience that shows that one-third will like the program, one-third will have no opinion, and one-third will dislike the program?

As an example of how goodness-of-fit testing is applied, suppose a new demographic theory predicts that in the population as a whole, four ethnic groups will occur in the proportions 9:3:3:1, and suppose also that a random sample of 240 persons was observed with 120, 40, 55, and 25 people in the four categories. Then a goodness-of-fit test might be applied to determine the compatibility between the theoretically expected and empirically observed data. The result of the test would be a chi square statistic which could be computed using the following table and formula:

Goodness-of-Fit Table

	Category 1	Category 2	. . .	Category n
Empirical Frequencies	o_1	o_2	. . .	o_n
Theoretical Frequencies	t_1	t_2	. . .	t_n

Chi Square Formula $= X^2 = \sum_{i=1}^{n} \dfrac{(o_i - t_i)^2}{t_i}$ where:

n = number of categories

o_i = obtained or empirical frequency for the ith category

t_i = theoretical or expected frequency for the ith category

---

If the obtained or empirical data (o_i) are the same as the theoretical data (t), there will be a perfect fit, and the difference ($o_i - t_i$) for each category will be zero and so will the chi square value. Consequently, the smaller the chi square value, the better the fit, and the larger the chi square value, the poorer the fit between the empirical and theoretical data. The computed chi square values can be compared to values in chi square tables so that the hypothesis about goodness of fit can be accepted or rejected at the desired level of statistical significance.

Contingency Tables   Contingency tables refer to a type of chi square analysis in which two sets of empirical data expressed as frequencies are compared. One situation that is amenable to analysis using contingency tables involves testing if a significant relationship exists between two variables. For example, the relationship between the proportion of students on probation and gender might be organized in a contingency table like the one below, and then analyzed using a chi square statistic.

Contingency Table for Testing the Relationship Between Variables

	Not on Probation	On Probation
Male	Number of Observations	Number of Observations
Female	Number of Observations	Number of Observations

Another situation for which contingency tables are appropriate involves determining whether two sets of empirical data are alike, or in mathematical terms, testing whether the two sets of observed data are random samples from the same population. For example, the number of children contracting polio in samples of vaccinated and not vaccinated children might be compared using a contingency table and a chi square statistic.

Contingency Tables

Contingency Table for Testing Differences Between Groups

	Not Vaccinated	Vaccinated
Polio	Number of Observations	Number of Observations
No Polio	Number of Observations	Number of Observations

The chi square statistic that is used for contingency tables is similar to the one used for goodness-of-fit tests. However, in this case, the observed frequencies rather than the theoretical frequencies are compared with expected frequencies (i.e. those that can be expected if the hypothesis of no relationship between variables or no differences between groups is true) rather than with theoretical frequencies.

EXAMPLE: CHI SQUARE

Program Description: The LEGAL Program is designed to help students pass the qualifying examination for law school. The program gives students practice in answering test questions like those found on standardized tests for admittance to law school. LEGAL will be considered meritorious if a significantly greater number of its graduates get accepted to law school than applicants who did not participate.

Evaluation Question: Is there a statistically significant difference between people who participate in LEGAL and those who do not in terms of their acceptance into law school?

Design Strategy: A comparison group design was used for the evaluation question. The data were organized into a contingency table with two variables, program participation (which was studied at two levels: program and no program), and admittance to law school (which was also being studied at two levels: not admitted and admitted).

Two hundred and ten college seniors were selected at random to participate in the evaluation from all the students who requested in September to enroll in LEGAL. Half the 210 students were then randomly selected to participate in the program, and the other half were refused. Two of the students who were refused enrollment in LEGAL were subsequently disqualified from the evaluation because they enrolled in another program similar in intent to LEGAL.

Evaluation Sample

No LEGAL	LEGAL
103	105

Analysis Plan: The data were organized into a contingency table, and a chi square statistic was used to test the hypothesis that the participants and nonparticipants were alike in terms of their law school admittance status.

Analysis Results:

	No LEGAL	LEGAL	Totals
Not Admitted	80	30	110
Admitted	23	75	98
Totals	103	105	208

Chi square value (X^2) = 48.4
Degrees of freedom = 1
Significance = $p < .01$

The results of the chi square statistical analysis indicate that the hypothesis that the participants and nonparticipants are alike can be rejected.

Interpretation: The chi square test resulted in a value of 48.4, indicating that there are statistically significant differences between people who participated in the LEGAL program and those who did not, with participants in LEGAL begin accepted to law school more frequently than nonparticipants.

CONDUCTING INFORMATION ANALYSIS ACTIVITIES
Pilot Testing the Information Analysis Activities

Analyzing evaluation information is more than just applying analytic methods. It involves all of the following activities:
- pilot testing the information analysis activities
- conducting the analyses
- interpreting the results of the analyses
- recording and storing the evaluation information

Information analysis activities must be pilot tested to determine whether they can be performed and, if not, to modify them so that they can.

A pilot test should include all the planned information analysis activities and should reveal whether:
1) the necessary information will be available in a manageable form;
2) enough information exists and it is good enough to apply the analysis methods;
3) special equipment like computers or expert personnel are available;
4) the data reduction procedures are efficient and accurate.

Conducting the Analyses

Once the information analysis activities have been pilot tested and revised, the evaluator can actually begin to analyze the information. Sometimes evaluation questions require more than one analysis; some should be performed only if the results of previous analyses warrant further investigation. As an example, consider an evaluation question that asks which of four different drugs is most effective for treating schizophrenia. A statistical method like a one-way analysis of variance could be used to answer the evaluation question by testing the hypothesis that there is no difference between the drugs in terms of their average effectiveness. If the results confirm the hypothesis then no further analysis would be warranted. If, on the other hand, the analysis disproves the hypothesis, indicating that there are differences between the drugs, additional analysis would be needed to determine which drug or drugs are responsible for the differences.

Although an ordered approach to information analysis is the most efficient, evaluators often have the notion that "the most analysis is the best analysis." However, any security gained from conducting all possible analyses is likely to be only temporary. A desultory approach to information analysis is technically unsound because more analyses bring with them an increased probability of finding significant results by chance alone. The resultant evaluation is also less credible because it is no longer based on a plan that has been specifically tailored to answer the evaluation questions. Finally, the approach is hopelessly inefficient, as anyone who has attempted to sort through an avalanche of findings can confirm.

Interpreting the Results of the Analyses

The results of information analysis are numbers, descriptions, explanations, justifications of events, and statistical statements. Interpreting the results means translating all these into meaningful terms by applying reasoned speculation to answer the evaluation questions. For example, suppose an evaluation question asks whether shoppers pay attention to the "price per pound" information printed on food containers, and suppose an analysis of a survey questionnaire revealed that 40% of the shoppers answered "yes." In interpreting this information to answer the evaluation question, the evaluator would have to consider these questions first:

- Is 40% sufficient to prove the program's effectiveness?
- Were the shoppers who responded to the survey representative of "all shoppers"?
- Does a positive response mean that shoppers really use price-per-pound information?

Underlying these questions are issues related to evidence of program merit, the evaluation's design strategy and sampling procedures, and the validity of information collection and analysis methods. If the evaluation has been well organized, these issues have been dealt with continuously, resulting in information that can be readily interpreted to answer the evaluation questions.

Once the analysis results have been interpreted to answer each evaluation question, they may then be considered collectively in order to look at the program as a whole. This second interpretation is useful to portray the dynamics of the program and the relationships among its components.

Another kind of interpretation involves distinguishing between statistical and programmatic significance. A statistically significant outcome is one that is unlikely to occur by chance and a programmatically significant outcome is one that is meaningful in terms of a program's goals. It can be helpful to view statistical and programmatic significance as analogues to reliability and validity. Like reliability, statistical significance is a measure of precision, and like validity, programmatic significance is a measure of the meaningfulness of an observation.

Statistical significance is usually determined as part of the data analysis process. It is not necessarily synonymous with programmatic significance. With very large numbers of people it is possible to obtain statistically significant outcomes which do not really represent gains in performance or changes in behavior that are important or meaningful results of a program. Students in a new Program A, for example, may learn, on the average, five more vocabulary words than students in traditional Program B and this difference might be statistically significant. However, the issue raised by programmatic significance is whether the difference provides sufficient evidence of merit to justify the development, implementation, and costs of Program A. In anticipation of the interpretation process, programmatic significance should be defined when evidence of program merit is discussed.

Finally, analysis results may also be interpreted to provide recommendations and offer suggestions about how to improve or certify the effectiveness of programs. The evaluator is not always expected to give recommendations, however, and the client is *never* obligated to use them.

Recommendations like those in the following example are most frequently requested by clients during improvement evaluations.

EXAMPLE: INTERPRETATION WITH RECOMMENDATIONS

An analysis using descriptive statistics found that Group 1 shoppers, who are between 20-40 years of age, have achieved the standards set for attention to price-per-pound information, while Group 2 shoppers, who are between 40-60 years of age, have not. It is therefore recommended that price-per-pound information continue to be provided in markets that serve young communities. It is also recommended that this information be provided for foodstuffs that are primarily purchased by young consumers.

The following guidelines are useful when making interpretations:

1. Be attentive to the information that is needed to answer the evaluation questions and provide evidence of program merit. In some cases, the analysis will provide much information, only a fraction of which is relevant to the evaluation questions or the evidence of program merit.
2. Don't try to extrapolate beyond the limits of the analysis results. Each analysis method is limited by assumptions about how the findings can be interpreted and used. For example, it is dangerous to generalize to a rural population findings based on an urban population. Remember that the existence of a strong relationship between two events or variables must not be interpreted to mean that one of them caused the other.
3. Be concerned with the quality of the evaluation information that is used in the analysis. Sometimes instruments used to collect information provide data that are of indeterminate or poor quality.
4. Be sensitive to personal bias, like wanting to see a program succeed or fail.

Recording and Storing the Evaluation Information

Evaluation information should be kept carefully and not thrown out or stored in some haphazard fashion. If the information collection and analysis activities are done properly, a great deal of time and money has been spent to obtain information that is accurate and meaningful, and it would be senseless to waste it. This information can be used to reproduce the evaluation findings if they are challenged, or it can be used by other evaluators and researchers to find out more about the program and how it works. Like personal income tax information, it is probably a good idea to store evaluation information for some period of time before discarding it.

Evaluation records can take several forms. For example, historians might prepare an annotated bibliography, ethnographers might catalog their field notes and videotapes, and educational psychologists might put all their data onto computer cards and prepare a code book.

The procedures used to record evaluation information should be discussed and, when possible, agreed upon by the client and the evaluator. In

EXAMPLE: AN EXCERPTED INFORMATION ANALYSIS PLAN FOR A HEALTH EDUCATION PROGRAM

Evaluation Questions	Description of the Design		Source of the Information	Analysis Methods	Limitations
Did students who participated in the program know significantly more about diseases at the end of the school year than comparable students who did not participate?	**Pre** / **Post** grid: Participants | Nonparticipants Independent variable: Program participation Covariate: Knowledge of diseases at the beginning of the program Dependent variable: Knowledge of diseases at the conclusion of the program		The New Health Achievement Test	ANCOVA (To check that ANCOVA is really needed, a one-way ANOVA will be conducted to determine if there are significant differences in pretest scores. If no significant differences are found, then a one-way ANOVA will be conducted to compare posttest scores without any adjustments.)	Must meet parallelism of regression lines requirement Must only use data from students who completed pretests and posttests
Did the number of students who acquired the amount of knowledge considered to be acceptable for their grade level increase?	Pre | Post grid Independent variable: Timing of measures Dependent variable: Knowledge		The New Health Achievement Test	One-way repeated measures ANOVA (or dependent t-test)	Must only use data from students who completed pretests and posttests
Did students use special curriculum materials that emphasized decision making and common adolescent and childhood diseases?	Case design Dependent variable: Use of curriculum materials		Archive review of curriculum materials	Descriptive statistics (to include frequency counts, and computation of means, ranges, standard deviations)	
Did students know significantly more about diseases at the end of the school year than they did at the beginning?	Pre | Post grid Independent variable: Timing of measures Dependent variable: Knowledge of diseases		The New Health Achievement Test	Repeated measures one-way ANOVA (or dependent t-test)	Must only use data from students who completed pretest and posttest

some cases, the client has legal ownership of the evaluation information. In other cases, the client has no interest in the information and the evaluator can use it at his or her discretion.

The Information Analysis Plan (IAP)

The IAP is a document that summarizes the analysis methods selected for the evaluation. For each evaluation question, it describes the design strategy, the source of the information to be analyzed, the analysis methods, and any limitations that can affect the analysis.

An example of an excerpted IAP for the evaluation of the health education program is on page 69.

It is a good idea to share the IAP with clients. They may offer suggestions or favor certain analysis methods, but many program directors and sponsors hesitate to offer opinions about the analysis methods since they are frequently considered the most technical and esoteric aspect of the evaluation. Therefore, the responsibility for developing the IAP rests with the evaluator. When the client chooses not to participate in planning the information analysis, the evaluator should have the information collection and analysis plans reviewed by experts. In fact, it is always a good idea to have these plans reviewed to protect the evaluator and clients. Reviews protect the evaluator against later claims of inappropriate or poorly defined information collection or analysis activities, and protect clients by confirming the quality of the evaluation's information collection or analysis plans.

CHAPTER 7

REPORTING EVALUATION INFORMATION

An evaluation report answers some or all of the evaluation questions and explains the procedures used to derive the answers. The evaluation report is the official record of the evaluation, making public the evaluator's activities and findings. If interested people are unable to gain access to or understand the report, then the evaluator has failed to fulfill a major responsibility. For this reason, it is very important to prepare the report carefully.

The evaluation report is usually written by the evaluator and his or her staff. Because clarity is important, the evaluator may seek the assistance of professional writers or editors who can take a draft version and make it more readable. The evaluation report should be believable, truthful, and easily understood. Since the report will be read by individuals with varying degrees of knowledge about the program and its evaluation, the evaluator must make sure that any willing reader can make sense of the findings. Nonstatisticians should be able to understand an evaluation's results even if it involved sophisticated information analyses, and statisticians should be able to find all relevant technical information.

Evaluation reports are often no more than directories of data accompanied by tables of statistics, computer printouts, pages of calculations without explanation. Such reports are without value.

It is the evaluator's responsibility to communicate in a comprehensible way—without omitting any qualitative or quantitative details—what was done, how it was done, and why it was done.

Evaluators who like statistics are not alone in producing unbelievable, unusable, or unreadable reports. Those who eschew statistics often rely on intuition and report only feelings or beliefs. Impressionistic evaluation reports are garnished with findings and excuses such as, "They feel good (or bad) about the program," or "Human behavior is ambiguous and not subject to precise (or imprecise) measurement." However, neither an embellished computer printout nor personal musings are acceptable substitutes for an evaluation report.

Evaluation reports can be issued at different times during an evaluation and in different ways. Depending upon the arrangement with the evaluation's sponsor, reports can be issued weekly, monthly, quarterly, annually, or on an as-needed basis. Usually, however, at least one written report is required at the conclusion of the evaluation. Reports may be formal or informal, written or oral. Sometimes the evaluation's sponsoring agency develops a form for the evaluator to complete, or specifies the information that must be included in all written reports. Sometimes the sponsor asks to be kept up to date by phone calls or brief notes. Besides a written report, the sponsor may ask the evaluator to give talks about the evaluation and its progress. As with written reports, oral evaluation reports can vary from formal to informal. All evaluation reports should be made available in a written form, even if they are originally presented in another way. The evaluator and client should agree in advance upon the deadlines for the evaluation report and the form which it should take.

CONTENT OF EVALUATION REPORTS

A credible evaluation report clearly and logically describes the evaluation questions as well as the procedures used to get the answers. Whether informal or formal, written or oral, the report should include:

- an introduction to the evaluation, the evaluation questions, and limitations on the scope of the evaluation
- the design strategy and sampling procedures for each evaluation question and the limitations on them
- the information collection techniques and instruments and their limitations, and field activities
- the methods used to analyze the evaluation information, their limitations, and the results for each analysis
- the answers to each evaluation question, including interpretations of findings and recommendations
- administrative details like schedules and staff assignments

The Introduction to an Evaluation Report

The introduction to the report should briefly describe the program or programs being evaluated, the group that is conducting the evaluation, and their approach to evaluation. This section of the report should discuss any legislation that created the program and mandated its evaluation. It should also include the process by which evaluator (and client) arrived at statements of program goals, activities, and evidence of program merit. Finally, an explanation of the choice of evaluation questions, a list of the questions and a description of any constraints imposed upon the scope of the evaluation should be given.

Reporting Design and Sampling

A report should describe the evaluation's design strategy and sampling procedures and any limitations on them. For each evaluation question, the evaluator should explain and justify the way participants were grouped, the independent and dependent variables, the sample, and any limitations on internal and external validity. A drawing of the design is also very helpful.

The discussion of the plan used to select participants for the evaluation should include the sampling procedure used (e.g., purposive sampling); the justification for any subdivisions or strata into which the population of potential participants was divided for sampling purposes; the final numbers of individuals in the sample; and any problems encountered in selecting the participants or limitations that are inherent in the sampling plan. Once again, giving a picture of the final sample is useful. Finally, it is important to discuss how well the procedures produced the desired sample, at least in so far as can be ascertained through statistical methods or comparisons with tables of demographic data.

Reporting Information Collection

The evaluation report should describe each instrument, the people to whom it was administered and when, and explain its appropriateness for answering the evaluation questions. The entire instrument should be reprinted if possible, and if not, sample items should be given. In some cases, instructions for obtaining the instrument might have to suffice if the instrument has been commercially published and is protected by copyright.

An evaluation report should also contain information about the reliability and validity of the instruments. Were they pilot-tested or validated? If so, with and by whom? What were the results? It is also a good idea to explain how the instrument was administered and scored.

The evaluation report must summarize all field activities, noting any irregularities in information collection that could affect the evaluation's findings. If interviewers strayed from the set procedures for interviewing, for example, then the report should describe what happened and what the consequences were. Finally, the evaluation report should state how many people participated in each information collection activity, for how many of them complete data were available, and give reasons for any missing information.

Information Analysis

For each separate analytic method, a description should be given of its relationship to the evaluation questions, the source of information for the analysis, the design strategy (including the independent and dependent variables) and any limitations. Also the analysis results and interpretations of the findings that relate them to the evaluation questions should be given for each analytic procedure. Finally, although the analyses need not be explained in terms of their mathematical or philosophical derivations, they must be named and justified. No matter how careful an evaluator may be, the quality of the methodology may be challenged because there are many equally appropriate procedures, each with its own advocates.

The Evaluation Findings

The most critical part of an evaluation report is the answers to the evaluation questions. The report must provide clear and succinct answers or describe the progress being made toward obtaining them. When reporting answers to evaluation questions, it is important to point out the strengths and weaknesses of the program. Clients who have been instrumental in developing or funding a program are likely to reject evaluation findings that are totally negative. On the other hand, individuals not directly involved with the program are likely to be suspicious of an evaluation report that is totally favorable. Of course, occasionally an evaluation will have only positive or only negative findings.

Recommendations sometimes accompany answers to evaluation questions, but not all clients ask for or want recommendations. Instead, they prefer to make their own. The evaluator should always find out in advance if recommendations are required, and if they are, how extensive they should be. When making recommendations, the evaluator should not assume the policy maker's responsibility of deciding whether or not to continue a program's funding. Instead, the evaluator should focus recommendations on how to improve the program, on the situations in which the program can achieve the best results, and on the individuals who are most likely to benefit from the program.

In answering the evaluation questions and in making recommendations, it is important to explain the limitations imposed upon the evaluation. For example, if information came from instruments whose reliability or validity is suspect, the reader should be reminded about it when the evaluation question is answered. The evaluator must report the limitations on the evaluation findings even if this makes the report appear noncommittal and the results more difficult to translate into policy or action. The evaluator's responsibility is fulfilled only if policy makers get credible and understandable answers they can use to make decisions.

Administration

An evaluation report should provide information about the sequence of events between defining the evaluation's questions and arriving at the answers. Information about the evaluation's staff may also be appropriate in this section of the report. One way to combine information about the evaluation schedule and staff is to draw up a calendar of events.

Evaluation Summary

Evaluation summaries take the activities and findings described in a relatively large evaluation report and distill them into a few pages. The purpose of the summary is to give people an overview of the evaluation that is easy to read but detailed enough to be believable and usable. The summary is frequently placed at the beginning of an evaluation report as a kind of introduction. It is a convenient device for informing the public about the program and its evaluation. Because it may be more widely distributed than the complete report, the evaluation summary must be carefully prepared. A good evaluation summary must be convincing to the busy or lazy reader as well as to the more available or energetic one. Unless the evaluator is absolutely certain of his or her ability to condense information in a meaningful and readable way, professional writers with training in journalism or technical writing should be employed to prepare the evaluation summary if funds permit.

A SAMPLE EVAL-UATION REPORT

Introduction

Excerpts from a sample evaluation report for the health education program follow. For brevity's sake, only those portions of the report that relate to a single evaluation question are given.

The Health Education Program was designed by the University Curriculum Laboratory in cooperation with the Medical Association. Its development was funded through Title A of the Elementary School Act of 1976, Part III. The general purpose of the program, as stated in the legislation, is "to help young children to understand and maintain good health."

The Health Education Program is now in its fourth year of operation. During the past academic year, the program was used in eight states by 24 school districts, 113 elementary schools, and over 26,000 children.

This evaluation was conducted by the State Department of Health, Education, and Welfare's Evaluation Unit. The purpose of the evaluation was to meet the legislative mandate to "certify the effectiveness of programs developed under Title A, Part III in terms of their impact on students' cognitive development, attitudes, and behavior."

The Fink and Kosecoff evaluation approach (1977) was used to guide the evaluation. Their approach involves ....

The Evaluator's Program Description

The evaluation team met three times with Dr. Avril Jones from the State Department of Health, Education, and Welfare, and twice with Mr. Cyril Morgan and Dr. Elizabeth Smith, the developers of the Health Education Program, to define the program's goals and activities and to decide on evidence of program merit. In addition, the team extensively reviewed the program proposal, curriculum materials, and past evaluation reports and visited three schools (Washington, Jefferson, and Lincoln Elementary Schools in the Kennedy Unified School District) to observe the program. From these activities came a draft of the Evaluator's Program Description (EPD). The draft was submitted for review to Dr. Jones , Mr. Morgan, Dr. Smith, and teachers at each of the three elementary schools in March, and based on their suggestions, a final EPD was prepared, reviewed, and approved on April 15, 1978. An excerpt of the completed EPD can be found in Figure 1.

FIGURE 1: THE EVALUATOR'S PROGRAM DESCRIPTION

Goals	*Activities*	*Evidence of Program Merit*
1.		
2. To increase students' knowledge about disease	Special health curriculum materials emphasizing common adolescent and childhood diseases are used.	• The use of special materials • Students demonstrate significantly more knowledge of diseases (i.e., their causes and symptoms, how they affect the body, and the ways in which they can be treated) than they did at the beginning of the program and more than comparable students who did not participate in the program. • An increase in the number of students who acquire the amount of knowledge considered to be acceptable for their grade level.
3.		

Using the EPD, the evaluation team drew up a set of evaluation questions and submitted them to all members of the Advisory Committee—Mr. Morgan, Dr. Smith, Dr. Jones, Mrs. Susan LaBella (a teacher at Jefferson Elementary School), and Dr. Ralph Stoner (a professor of medical education at Harvard University). An excerpt from the final set of evaluation questions, approved on May 21, 1978, can be found in Table 1.

The Evaluation Questions

TABLE 1: THE EVALUATION QUESTIONS

1.
2.
3.
4.   Did students in the experimental program know significantly more about diseases at the end of the school year than they did at the beginning?
5.
6.

Evaluation of the Health Education Program was restricted by the Advisory Committee to questions that must be answered under a strict interpretation of the legislation, ignoring other important questions that might have been asked about the program. For example, the evaluation did

not ask about the program's impact on the morale or self concept o.
children and their parents.

The Sample   The Kennedy Unified School District, the largest district in the state, wa:
selected to participate in the evaluation. In each of the district's 32 elementary
schools, one third-grade classroom was selected at random for the
experimental health program, and one third-grade classroom was selected a'
random not to receive any health education program. The remaining
classrooms were allowed to continue with their regular health education
program, if one existed. The sample is depicted in Figure 2.

FIGURE 2: THE EVALUATION SAMPLE					
	School 1	School 2	. . . . . .	School 32	Total
Experimental Program	1 classroom	1 classroom	. . . . . .	1 classroom	32 classrooms
No Program (Control)	1 classroom	1 classroom	. . . . . .	1 classroom	32 classrooms
Total	2 classrooms	2 classrooms	. . . . . .	2 classrooms	64 classrooms

The sample selected to participate in the evaluation was compared to all
third-grade students in Kennedy Unified School District in terms of students'
age, reading and mathematics ability, and ethnic and sex composition, and
teachers' years of experience, sex, and ethnicity. The results of a series of
chi square tests showed that there were no significant differences between
the sample and all third-grade students

Design   The design strategy used to group students is described separately for each
evaluation question. . .

Evaluation Question 4: Did students in the experimental program know
significantly more about diseases at the end of the school year than they
did at the beginning?

To answer this question, a time series design was used. The independent
variable was the timing of measures (which was studied at two levels:
preinstruction and postinstruction) and the dependent variable was knowledge of diseases. All classrooms in the experimental program were included
in the design which can be illustrated as follows:

Preinstruction	Postinstruction

The limitations on the internal validity of the design include history (some
event like the public television series on the microbe hunters might have
influenced students' knowledge); maturation (during the school year
students may have matured and in so doing, may have learned more about
their bodies' health and disease); testing (taking the preinstruction measure
may have affected students' performance on the postinstruction measure,
although different forms of the measures were used on each occasion); and
instrumentation (the administration procedures may have differed from time
to time).

76

Limitations on the design's external validity include the reactive effects of testing (the preinstruction measure may have alerted students to their lack of knowledge about diseases, making them more attentive to the program); the interactive effects of selection bias (students in this program may not be representative of students in other districts); the reactive effects of innovation (the fact that students were in a special program might have motivated them to learn); multiple program interference (some of the students also participated in a compensatory education program at the same time as the health education program, and it was not possible to distinguish the effects of one program from the other.

Information Collection

For each question, the evaluation team selected one or more information collection techniques that were likely to provide answers. The proposed information collection techniques were submitted to the Advisory Committee for review. Figure 3 contains an excerpt from the approved Evaluation Questions with Information Collection Techniques document and summarizes any limitations.

Evaluation Questions	Information Collection Technique(s) To Be Used	Limitations			
		Schedule	Design	Sampling	Other
1.					
2.					
3.					
4. Did students in the experimental program know significantly more about diseases at the end of the school year than they did at beginning?	Paper and Pencil Achievement Test		Must have parallel forms of the achievement test	All program participants must be tested	Must insure confidentiality of responses
5.					
6.					

FIGURE 3: THE EVALUATION QUESTIONS WITH INFORMATION COLLECTION TECHNIQUES

Once the information collection techniques were agreed upon, the evaluation team began to select, adapt, or develop the appropriate instruments. Each of these instruments will now be discussed....

The New Health Achievement Test

To answer the question about students' knowledge of diseases, the evaluation team chose the New Health Achievement Test (NHAT) because it was specially designed to measure elementary school students' knowledge of health problems and how to manage them. The NHAT was developed by the National Institutes for Health Education and is available from them. The NHAT is a self-administered test and takes approximately 30 minutes for students to complete.

This instrument has been validated on over 6,000 elementary-school children within the last five years.... Split-half reliability of .89 and test-retest reliability of .98 were reported on the average for third-grade students.... Content validity was established through expert review by over 100 educators and health professionals....

Scores are reported on a scale of 1 to 50.... Norm tables are available for third-grade students as a group and divided by sex, ethnicity, and geographic location....

Information collection was scheduled to take place between October 1, 1978 and May 30, 1979. A summary of the information collection plan is given in Figure 4.

FIGURE 4: THE INFORMATION COLLECTION PLAN			
Specific Information Collection Technique(s) (Instruments)	Time and Place for Information Collection	Nature of the Sample for the Technique	Who Will Collect the Information
New Health Achievement Test (NHAT): Forms A and B	The first week in October and the last week in May in students' regular classrooms.	All students in third-grade classrooms receiving the program and all students in third-grade classrooms not receiving any program.	Teachers will be trained to administer the tests, and the evaluation team will monitor the process.

FIGURE 5: INFORMATION ANALYSIS PLAN				
Evaluation Questions	Description of the Design	Source of the Information	Analysis Methods	Limitations
1.				
2.				
3.				
4. Did students in the experimental progam know significantly more about diseases at the end of the school year than they did at the beginning?	Pre | Post □□ Independent variable: Timing of measures Dependent variable: Knowledge of diseases.	The New Health Achievement Test: Forms A and B	Dependent t-test or one-way repeated measures analysis of variance.	Must use data only from students who completed pretests and posttests.
5.				

Field Activities

....Form A of the New Health Achievement Test (NHAT) was given to all students in the 32 classrooms in the program on October 2, 1978. Of 928 possible students, only 17 students were absent or did not complete the test. Form B was given to all students who took a preinstruction test on May 25,

1979. Of the 911 possible students, 53 were absent or had moved and another 10 did not finish the test. Consequently, complete data for the NHAT were available for 848 students in the 32 classrooms participating in the experimental program.

Form A was administered to all students in the 32 control classrooms on October 2, 1978....

Teachers and evaluation staff reported no administrative problems.

Information Analysis

The evaluation team selected appropriate analysis methods for each evaluation question and submitted the proposed information analysis plan to Dr. Harold Schwartz, Professor of Biostatistics and Evaluation at Stanford University and to the Advisory Committee. Based on this review, a final analysis plan was prepared and approved. An excerpt is depicted in Figure 5, on page 78.

Analysis Results

The results of each separate analysis are presented in this section of the report....

A dependent t-test was conducted to find out how much students learned about diseases as a result of their participation in the experimental health education program. The independent variable for the analysis was time of testing, which was investigated at two levels: pre and postinstruction. The dependent variable was students' knowledge as represented by scores on Form A (preinstruction) and Form B (postinstruction) of the New Health Achievement Test (NHAT), which focuses on knowledge of symptoms of diseases, how diseases affect the body, and the ways in which they can be treated. The unit of analysis was the classroom mean, and the hypotheses tested by the analysis were:

Null hypothesis: Preinstruction mean score = Postinstruction
mean score
Alternate hypothesis: Preinstruction mean score < Postinstruction
mean score

The results of the analyses are given in Table 2.

TABLE 2: RESULTS OF t-TEST FOR NHAT							
Time of Testing	Mean* Score	Standard Deviation	Number of Cases	Corre-lation	t-Value	Degrees of Freedom	One-Tailed Significance
Preinstruction Form A	36.32	7.01	32	.75	5.76	31	<.01
Postinstruction Form B	41.41	6.85					

*Total possible score = 50 points

Table 2 shows that the t-value is significant, indicating that the increase in students' knowledge was statistically meaningful.

Students in the experimental program did learn about diseases.

The Evaluation Findings

In this section of the report, answers to each evaluation question are given....

Evaluation Question 4: Did students in the experimental program know significantly more about diseases at the end of the school year than they did at the beginning?

A dependent t-test was conducted to determine if students' knowledge about diseases increased as a result of their participation in the experimental program. The 5.09 preinstruction to postinstruction gain was found to be statistically significant, suggesting that the answer to Question 4 is yes.

Administration

Table 3 summarizes the evaluation schedule.

TABLE 3: EVALUATION SCHEDULE	
October 19, 1977	Meeting with Dr. _____ and others from the Office of _____....
October 31, 1977	Proposal for Evaluation Study of _____ submitted to the Office of _____....
November 20, 1977	Revised evaluation design submitted to Dr. _____ at the District Office of _____....
June 30, 1978	Sampling procedures refined and implemented....
July 31, 1979	Data analysis completed....
August 15, 1979	Preliminary draft of final report completed....
August 31, 1979	Submission of Final Report to State Department of Health, Education and Welfare....
September 1, 1979	Thank you letter sent to all participants in the evaluation study....

CHAPTER 8
MANAGING AN EVALUATION

Evaluation information is perishable. Unless clients get timely and usable answers to their questions, the evaluation isn't worth much. The ability to coordinate evaluation activities so that the right information is ready when needed is essential. Three primary management functions are important to evaluation: establishing schedules, assigning staff and monitoring their activities, and budgeting.

Evaluations are expected to be completed within a given amount of time. If the evaluation is not finished within the allotted time, additional funds are not provided unless special arrangements are made. Consequently, the evaluator must decide when each evaluation activity will take place, the sequence of activities, and how long each activity will last. Establishing evaluation schedules requires attention to:
- the evaluation activities themselves
- the deadline for completing each activity
- the amount of time to be given to each activity

The *activities* performed during evaluations involve getting to know the program's goals and activities and generating evaluation questions; developing the evaluation design strategy and sampling procedures; planning and conducting information collection and analysis; and reporting evaluation information. The *deadline for completing each activity* refers to the date by which the activity is expected to be accomplished. *The amount of time to be given to each activity* is the actual number of hours, days or weeks that will be devoted to the activity, and it is usually computed on the basis of time spent by professional staff. Developing a questionnaire might require two weeks of work, but the ten working days may be spread out over a two-month period.

The evaluation activities, deadlines, and time allocations are usually scheduled by the evaluator, although some or all can be specified in advance by the client. For example, the client might ask for two progress reports and one final report, due on certain dates. Evaluation activities, deadlines, and time allocations can be combined in several ways to create schedules. The following are examples of schedules used in managing the evaluations of the health education program.

ESTABLISHING SCHEDULES

Activities	Dates	Time Allocation (Total Days)
1. Becoming familiar with the program goals, activities, and evidence of program merit, including: • reading all program-related documents and reports • meeting with program director and staff • observing program operation	March 1, 1978 to April 15, 1978	15
2. Formulating evaluation questions, including a review by program staff and Advisory Committee	April 16, 1978 to May 31, 1978	10
3. Preparing evaluation design strategies and sampling plan	June 1, 1978 to June 30, 1978	10
4. Preparing information collection to include field testing	June 15, 1978 to September 30, 1978	12
5. Collecting evaluation information	October 1, 1978 to May 30, 1979	35
6. Preparing information for analysis	November 1, 1978 to June 15, 1979	7
7. Analyzing evaluation information and interpreting the results, including a review of findings by the program staff and Advisory Committee	February 1, 1979 to July 31, 1979	14
8. Preparing preliminary evaluation reports	August 30-31, 1978 February 27-28, 1979	4
9. Preparing final evaluation report	June 1, 1979 to August 31, 1979	22

EXAMPLE: SAMPLE EVALUATION SCHEDULE*

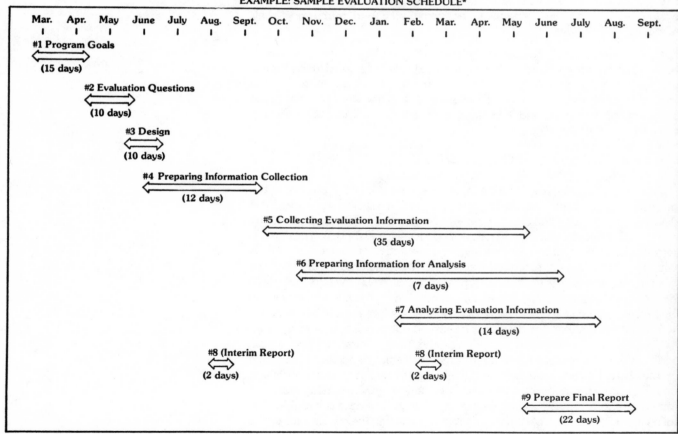

*The numbers in the parentheses refer to the amount of professional staff time allocated to each activity.

The first example lists a beginning and an ending date (or deadline) for each activity and specifies the time allocated to it. The format used can be easily expanded to include other management considerations such as staff assignments. The second example is a graphic representation of a time schedule organized by months. Beginning and ending dates for each activity are joined by an arrowed line and the amount of days allocated to each activity is placed in parentheses directly under the line.

The evaluator should decide what skills are needed to perform each activity, so that the staff members with those skills can be assigned appropriately. The following example shows a convenient way to summarize staff assignments. It is an expansion of the example on page 82, enlarged to include columns of information pertaining to the specific amount of time allocated to each staff member for each activity.

ASSIGNING STAFF AND MONITORING ACTIVITIES

EXAMPLE: SAMPLE OVERVIEW OF ACTIVITIES, DATES, STAFF, AND TIME ALLOCATIONS

Activities	Dates	Staff Assignments	Time Allocated	
			By Staff	Total Days
1. Becoming familiar with the program's goals, activities, and evidence of program merit, including: • reading all program-related documents and reports • meeting with program director and staff • observing program in operation	March 1, 1978 to April 15, 1978	Smith Ramirez Goldberg	10 2 3	15
2. Formulating evaluation questions, including a review by program staff and Advisory Committee	April 16, 1978 to May 31, 1978	Smith Ramirez Goldberg	7 2 1	10
3. Preparing evaluation design strategies and sampling plan	June 1, 1978 to June 30, 1978	Smith Goldberg Cheung	2 7 1	10
4. Preparing information collection, including field testing	June 15, 1978 to September 30, 1978	Smith Ramirez Goldberg Cheung	2 1 6 3	12
5. Collecting evaluation information	October 1, 1978 to May 30, 1979	Smith Ramirez Goldberg	3 12 20	35
6. Preparing information for analysis	November 1, 1978 to June 15, 1979	Smith Ramirez	1 6	7
7. Analyzing evaluation information and interpreting the results, including review of findings by the program staff and Advisory Committee	February 1, 1979 to July 31, 1979	Smith Ramirez	3 11	14
8. Preparing preliminary evaluation reports	August 30-31, 1978 February 27-28, 1979	Smith	4	4
9. Preparing final evaluation report	June 1, 1979 to August 31, 1979	Smith Ramirez Goldberg Cheung	7 6 6 3	22

BUDGETING

Managing an evaluation also means keeping an eye on how efficiently the staf performs the evaluation activities. Information must therefore be collectec that describes the amount of time spent on each activity, how thoroughl each activity has been accomplished, and any problems encountered. Thi information can be collected in a variety of ways, ranging from highl structured reporting systems to informal meetings with staff members.

An evaluation usually has a given amount of money and must b accomplished without exceeding that amount. To prepare the budget, th evaluator must weigh what needs to be done against the available resource juggling activities, time allocations, and staff assignments according to th amount of money and time available.

Evaluation budgets vary in form and detail. Sometimes the format for budget is laid out ahead, and other times the evaluator is permitted to desig his or her own budget. The following budget for the health education progran contains many of the items required by state and federal agencies as well a by foundations which support health, education and welfare programs. Th budget distinguishes between direct and indirect costs. Direct costs are staf and non-staff costs related to a particular evaluation. For example, th salaries and expenses of secretaries or clerks who work for the evaluation ar charged as direct costs according to the amount of time actually spent on th evaluation. Indirect costs, on the other hand, are expenses that are no directly related to the particular evaluation but that contribute to th evaluation agency's continued existence. Secretaries or clerks who provid support services related to general administration or accounting would hav their expenses incorporated into the indirect costs.

The Health Education Program's Evaluation Budget

DIRECT COSTS

Direct costs are divided into staff and non-staff sections.

I. Staff

  A. Salaries and Wages

    This category lists the salaries and wages of full-time and part-time persons employed for the evaluation at a rate proportionate to thei efforts. For each staff position, the following information can be provided: number of persons at that position, their title, daily, monthl or annual salary, percent of time on the evaluation, number of month employed, and the total dollar figure.

EXAMPLE:

A. Salary and Wages

1. Dr. Peter Smith, Evaluation Director (39 days at $125 per diem)	$4,875
2. Dr. Barbara Ramirez, Information Analysis (35 days at $81.81 per diem)	$2,863
3. Dr. Robert Goldberg, Instrumentation (29 days at $88.64 per diem)	$2,571
4. Mr. Paul Cheung, Information Collection (26 days at $56.82 per diem)	$1,477
5. Secretary/Clerical Assistant (20% at $9,000 per annum, 3/1/78-8/31/79)	$2,700
Subtotal	**$14,486**

B. Employee Benefits

This category contains the costs of all employee benefits related to the salaries and wages of full-time or part-time staff. Benefits are usually computed as a percentage of salary and wages and include funds set aside by the employer for social security, retirement, medical care, etc. Sometimes each benefit is listed separately.

EXAMPLE:

B. Employee Benefits

    1. 20% of Salaries and Wages ($14,486)   **$2,897**

C. Consultants

Consultants are persons who are hired on an as-needed basis, such as reviewers, members of an advisory panel, subject matter experts, or field information collectors.

EXAMPLE:

C. Consultants

    1. Members of the Advisory Panel   **$900**
       (3 persons at $150 per diem for 2 days each)

II. Non-Staff

A. Rent

This category consists of the cost of using facilities for the evaluation and usually includes utilities and maintenance services.

EXAMPLE:

A. Rent

    1. Office space (120 sq.ft. at 45¢ per sq.ft. =   **$972**
       $54 per month for 18 months)

B. Office Supplies

This category lists consumable supplies used exclusively for the project, like paper, typewriter ribbons, etc.

EXAMPLE:

B. Office Supplies

    1. Office supplies (paper, etc.) at $16 per month   **$270**
       for 18 months

C. Equipment

This category specifies the cost of equipment acquired or rented for specific use on the project, like typewriters, photocopy machines, etc.

EXAMPLE:

C. Equipment

    1. Rental of typewriters and photocopy machines at   **$486**
       $27 per month for 18 months

D. Computer Use

This category lists computer time and necessary supporting services.

EXAMPLE:

D. Computer Use

    1. Computer time at $432 per hour   **$216**
    2. Data processing costs (tape, cards,   **$110**
       keypunching, etc.)

E. Telephone and Mail

This category lists costs of telephone services, phone calls, and postage directly related to the project.

EXAMPLE:

E. Telephone and Mail

    1. Telephone and mail at $18 per month   **$324**

        for 18 months

F. Printing and Reproduction

This category lists costs of photocopying, typesetting, duplicating reports, etc.

EXAMPLE:

F. Printing and Reproduction

    1. Printing (questionnaires, observation   **$1,200**

        schedules, reports)

    2. Reproduction at $5 per month for 18 months   **$90**

G. Travel

All travel charges that are directly incurred for the project including the per diem expenses, gas mileage, airfare.

EXAMPLE:

G. Travel

    1. Local travel, 300 miles at 15¢ per mile   **$45**

INDIRECT COSTS

Indirect costs are usually computed as a percent of the total direct costs or as a percent of salaries and wages.

EXAMPLE:

INDIRECT COSTS

    22% of Direct Costs ($21,996)   **$4,839**

These examples are translated into two commonly used budget formats on pages 87 and 88.

EXAMPLE 1: SAMPLE BUDGET

DIRECT COSTS

I. **Staff**
    A. Salaries and Wages.
        1. Dr. Peter Smith, Evaluation Director $ 4,875
           (39 days at $125 per diem)
        2. Dr. Barbara Ramirez, Information Analysis $ 2,863
           (35 days at $81.81 per diem)
        3. Dr. Robert Goldberg, Instrumentation $ 2,571
           (29 days at $88.64 per diem)
        4. Mr. Paul Chueng, Information Collection $ 1,477
           (26 days at $56.82 per diem)
        5. Secretary/Clerical Assistant $ 2,700
           (20% at $9,000 per annum 3/1/78–8/31/79)

                        Subtotal $ 14,486

    B. Employee Benefits
        1. 20% of Salaries and Wages ($14,486) $ 2,897

    C. Consultants
        1. Members of Advisory Board $ 900
           (3 persons at $150 per diem for 2 days each)

II. **Non-Staff**
    A. Rent
        1. Office Space, 120 sq.ft. at 45¢ per sq.ft. $ 972
           = $54 per month for 18 months

    B. Office Supplies
        1. Office Supplies (paper, etc.) at $15 per $ 270
           month for 18 months

    C. Equipment
        1. Rental of Typewriters and Photocopy $ 486
           Machine at $27 per month for 18 months

    D. Computer Use
        1. Computer Time at $432 per hour $ 216
        2. Data Processing costs (tape, cards,
           keypunching, etc.) $ 110

    E. Telephone and Mail
        1. Telephone and Mail at $18 per month
           for 18 months $ 324

    F. Printing and Reproduction
        1. Printing (questionnaires, observation $ 1,200
           schedules, reports)
        2. Reproduction at $5 per month for 18 months $ 90

    G. Travel
        1. Local Travel, 300 miles at 15¢ per mile $ 45

              Subtotal   (Direct Costs) $ 21,996

INDIRECT COSTS
    22% of Direct Costs ($21,996)
              Subtotal   (Indirect Costs) $ 4,839

                  TOTAL $ 26,835

EXAMPLE 2: SAMPLE BUDGET

Detailed Budget for 18-month Evaluation From 3/1/78 to 8/31/79

Personnel

Name	Title	Time	Salary	Benefits	Total
Dr. Peter Smith	Director	39 days	$4,875	$974	$5,850
Dr. Barbara Ramirez	Information Analysis	35 days	2,863	573	3,436
Dr. Robert Goldberg	Instrumentation	29 days	2,571	514	3,085
Mr. Paul Cheung	Information Collection	26 days	1,477	295	1,772
Secretary/Clerk	Secretary I	20%	2,700	540	3,240
	Subtotals		$14,486	$2,897	$17,383

Consultants

Members of the Advisory Committee, 3 persons
at $150 per diem for 2 days each   900

Equipment

Rental of typewriters and photocopy machine
at $27 per month   486

Supplies

Office Supplies (paper, etc.) at $15 per month   270

Travel

Local Travel, 300 miles at 15¢ per mile   45

Other

Rent (120 sq.ft. at 43¢ per sq.ft.)   972
Computer Time at $432 per hour   216
Data Processing Costs (tape, cards, keypunching)   110
Telephone and Mail at $18 per month   324
Printing (questionnaires, observation
schedules, reports)   120
Reproduction at $5 per month   90

	Subtotal	$ 1,832
22% Indirect Costs		4,839
	TOTAL	$ 26,835

Most clients require the evaluator to submit a written proposal describing how the evaluation will be conducted and managed. The evaluation proposal is usually modified as a result of negotiations between the evaluator and client, and the modified proposal becomes the contract between the evaluator and the client or the basis for a grant from the client to the evaluator.* Evaluation proposals must be as realistic as possible since the evaluator may become legally obligated to meet their specifications.

Sometimes the client provides a document called a Request for Proposal (RFP) that describes the prospective evaluation and tells what the evaluator should include in the proposal. RFPs are usually sent to several evaluation groups who are invited to submit proposals. The agency or program that issued the RFP then selects the "best" proposal and awards the contract.

The following example shows an annotated table of contents from a sample proposal.

EVALUATION PROPOSALS

EXAMPLE: ANNOTATED TABLE OF CONTENTS FOR AN EVALUATION PROPOSAL

Introduction
   Background—Social and historical circumstances that created the program and lend significance to its evaluation.
   Key Features—Special features of the proposed evaluation (e.g., unique resources and facilities or a unique methodology)

Review of the Literature—**Discussion of the professional literature that justifies and explains the significance of the evaluation model, the hypotheses or questions being addressed, and the proposed methodology.**

Technical Approach
   Overview—Description of the evaluation questions and brief outline of all information collection, analysis, and reporting activities that constitute the proposed evaluation.

Evaluation Questions—**The Evaluator's Program Description and an explanation of how the questions were derived.**

Design and Sampling—**A description of how individuals will be selected to participate in the proposed evaluation and how they will be grouped to answer each question.**

Information Collection—**A description of the proposed information collection plan, including the identity of any instruments that are proposed for use; how other instruments will be selected or developed; when each instrument will be administered; who will administer it; how instruments will be field tested; and the relationship between the information collection plan and the evaluation questions.**

Information Analysis—**A description of the analysis methods that will be used to answer the evaluation questions, including an example of at least one analysis and the interpretation of its findings.**

---

*Grants are a special form of contract. The decision as to whether a proposal will be a grant or a contract is made by the agency awarding the money and not by the evaluator.

Reporting—A description of the contents of reports and the dates they will be submitted.

Task-by-Task Description of the Evaluation Activities—The name of each activity, the individuals who will be responsible for its completion, and the times during which the activity will take place.

Quality Control—A description of how the evaluation will be monitored and how requirements for confidentiality of data will be maintained.

Administration—An explanation of staffing and scheduling and other administrative considerations.

Management—The identity of the prime contractor and any subcontractor and the relationship between them.

Statement of Qualifications—A description of the overall experience, capabilities, and related contracts/grants for each contractor or grantee, and a description of key staff members' experience and capabilities.

Appendixes

All materials that are supplemental to the proposal that cannot be included without breaking the continuity of thought, including

Sample information collection instruments
Staff resumes
Letters of commitment (to participate in the evaluation)

Costs

A detailed budget. Sometimes these costs are put into a document that is judged independently from the other parts of the proposal.

BIBLIOGRAPHY

GENERAL EVALUATION

Alkin, Marvin C.; Kosecoff, Jacqueline; Fitzgibbon, Carol; and Seligman, Richard. *Evaluation and Decision Making: The Title VII Experience.* CSE Monograph series in Evaluation, no. 4. Los Angeles: Center for the Study of Evaluation, University of California, 1974.

Anderson, Scarvia B.; Ball, Samuel; Murphy, Richard T. et al. *Encyclopedia of Educational Evaluation.* San Francisco: Jossey-Bass, Publishers, 1975.

Bloom, Benjamin S.; Hastings, J. Thomas; and Madaus, George F. *Handbook on Formative and Summative Evaluation of Student Learning.* New York: McGraw-Hill, Inc., 1971.

Caro, Francis G., ed. *Readings in Evaluation Research.* New York: Russell Sage Foundation, 1971.

Cronbach, Lee J. and Suppes, Patrick. *Research for Tomorrow's Schools: Disciplined Inquiry for Education.* New York: Macmillan, 1969.

Donabedian, Avedis. *Benefits in Medical Care Programs.* Cambridge: Harvard University Press, 1976.

Fink, Arlene and Kosecoff, Jacqueline. *Evaluating Federal Education Programs.* Washington, D.C.: Capitol Publications, Inc., 1976.

Freeman, Howard E. and Sherwood, Clarence C. "Research in Large-Scale Intervention Programs." *Journal of Social Issues* 21 (1965): 11-28.

Guttentag, Marcia and Struening, Elmer L. *Handbook of Evaluation Research.* Beverly Hills: Sage Publications, 1975.

House, Ernest L., ed. *School Evaluation.* Berkeley: McCutchan, 1973.

Lewis, Charles E.; Fein, Rashi; and Mechanic, David. *A Right to Health.* New York: John Wiley & Sons, Inc., 1976.

Popham, W. James, ed. *Evaluation in Education: Current Applications.* Berkeley: McCutchan Publishing Corporation, 1974.

Riecker, Henry W. and Boruch, Robert F., eds. *Social Experimentation: A Method for Planning and Evaluating Social Intervention.* New York: Academic Press, Inc. 1974.

Rossi, Peter H. and Williams, Walter. *Evaluating Social Programs.* New York: Seminar Press, 1972.

Schulberg, Herbert C.; Sheldon, Alan; and Baker, Frank. *Program Evaluation in the Health Fields.* New York: Behavioral Publications, 1969.

Suchman, Edward A. *Evaluative Research; Principles and Practice in Public Service and Social Action Programs.* New York: Russell Sage Foundation, 1967.

Walberg, Herbert, ed. *Evaluating Educational Performance.* Berkeley: McCutchan Publishing Corporation, 1974.

Weiss, Carol H. *Evaluating Action Programs.* Boston: Allyn & Bacon, Inc., 1972.

_____. *Evaluation Research.* Englewood Cliffs, N.J.: John Wiley & Sons, Inc. 1972.

Williams, Walter. *Social Policy Research and Analysis.* New York: Elsevier, 1971.

DEVELOPMENT, VALIDATION AND SELECTION OF EVALUATION MEASURES

American Psychological Association, *Standards for Educational ar Psychological Tests and Manuals.* Washington, D.C.: American Psycholo ical Association, 1966.

Beatty, Walcott, H., ed. *Improving Educational Assessment and c Inventory of Measures of Affective Behavior.* Washington, D.C.: Associ tion of Supervision and Curriculum Development, NEA, 1969.

Bracht, Glena H.; Hopkins, Kenneth D.; and Stanley, Julian C., eds. *Pe spectives in Educational and Psychological Measurement.* Englewoo Cliffs, N.J.: Prentice-Hall, Inc. 1972.

Brook, Robert H. and Avery, Allyson D. *Quality of Medical Car Assessment Using Outcome Measures: Executive Summary.* Sant Monica: Rand, August, 1976.

Brook, Robert H. and Avery, Allyson D. *Quality of Medical Care Assessmer Using Outcome Measures: Executive Summary.* Santa Monica: Ranc August, 1976.

Buros, Oscar K. *Mental Measurements Yearbooks.* Highland Parl N.J.:Gryphon Press, 1938, 1940, 1949, 1953, 1965, 1972.

Campbell, Donald C. and Fiske, Donald W. "Convergent and Discriminar Validation by the Multitrait-Multimethod Matrix." *Psychological Bulletin 5* (1959): 81-105.

Comrey, Andrew L.; Backer, Thomas E.; and Glaser, Edward H. . *Sourcebook for Mental Health Measures.* Washington, D.C.: Nation: Institute of Mental Health, 1973.

Crombach, Lee J. *Essentials of Psychological Testing.* 3rd ed. New Yorl Harper & Row, Publishers, Inc. 1970.

Ebel, Robert L. *Essentials of Educational Measurement.* Englewood Cliff: N.J.: Prentice-Hall, Inc. 1972.

Edwards, A.L. *Techniques of Attitude Scale Construction.* Englewood Cliff: N.J.: Prentice-Hall, Inc. 1957.

Gronlund, Norman E. *Constructing Achievement Tests.* Englewood Cliff: N.J.:Prentice-Hall, Inc. 1968.

_____*1. Measurement and Evaluation in Teaching.* 2nd ed. New York Macmillan, 1971

Harris, C.W.; Alkin, M.C.; and Popham, W.J., eds. *Perspectives in Criter ion-Referenced Measurement.* CSE Monograph Series in Evaluation, no.3 Los Angeles; Center for the Study of Evaluation, University of California 1974.

Hoepfner, Ralph, et al. *CSE-ECRC Preschool/Kindergarten Test Evalua tions.* Los Angeles: Center for the Study of Evaluation, University of Califor nia, 1971.

Hoepfner, Ralph, et al. *CSE Elementary School Test Evaluations.* Los Angeles: Center for the Study of Evaluation, University of California, 1970

Hoepfner, Ralph, et al. *CSE-RBS Test Evaluations: Tests of Higher Order Cognitive, Affective, and Interpersonal Skills.* Los Angeles: Center for the Study of Evaluation, University of California, 1972.

Hoepfner, Ralph, et al. *CSE Secondary Test Evaluations.* Los Angeles: Center for the Study of Evaluation, University of California, 1973.

Kahn, R.L. and Cannell, C.F. *The Dynamics of Interviewing: Theory, Techniques and Uses.* New York: Wiley & Sons, Inc. 1957.

Kaplan, Sherrie; Greenfield, Sheldon; and Klein, Bonnie. *User's Guide to the UCLA EMCRO Criteria Mapping System*. Los Angeles: University of California, 1976.

Kosecoff, Jacqueline, and Fink, Arlene. "The Appropriateness of Criterion-Referenced Tests for Evaluation Studies." *ERIC Clearinghouse on Tests, Measurement, and Evaluation,* Report 60. Princeton: Educational Testing Service, 1976.

Kosecoff, Jacqueline; Fink, Arlene; and Kaplan, Sherrie. *MAPS Abstractor Training Workshop—UCLA Criteria Mapping System*. Los Angeles: University of California, 1976.

Kosecoff, Jacqueline and Fink, Arlene. "A System for Describing and Evaluating Criterion-Referenced Tests." *ERIC Clearinghouse on Tests, Measurement, and Evaluation,* Report 57. Princeton: Educational Testing Service, 1976.

Lake, Dale G.; Miles, Mathew B.; and Earle, Ralph B., Jr., eds. *measuring Human Behavior*. New York: Teachers College Press, Columbia University, 1973.

Simon, A. and Boyer, E.G., eds. *Mirrors for Behavior: An Anthology of Classroom Observation Instruments*. Philadelphia: Research for Better Schools, 1968.

Srogjen, D.D. "Measurement Techniques in Evaluation." *Review of Educational Research* 40 (1970): 301-320.

INFORMATION ANALYSIS, SAMPLING, AND RESEARCH DESIGN

Boruch, Robert F. "Relations Among Statistical Methods for Assuring Confidentiality of Data." *Social Science Research* 1 (1972): 403-414.

Campbell, Donald T. and Stanley, Julian C. *Experimental and Quasi-Experimental Designs for Research*. Chicago: Rand McNally & Co., 1966.

Cochran, William G. *Sampling Techniques*. New York: John Wiley & Sons, Inc. 1953.

Daniel, W.W. *Biostatistics; A Foundation for Analysis in the Health Sciences*. New York: John Wiley & Sons, Inc. 1974.

Fleiss, Joseph L. *Statistical Methods for Rates and Proportions*. New York: John Wiley & Sons, Inc. 1973.

Glass, Gene V.; Willson, Victor L.; and Gottman, J.H. *Design and Analysis of Times-Series Experiments*. Boulder, CO.: Laboratory of Educational Research, University of Colorado, 1972.

Hess, Irene; Riedel, Donald, C.; and Fitzpatrick, T.B. *Probability Sampling of Hospitals and Patients*. Ann Arbor: Health Administration Press, 1975.

Kish, L. *Survey Sampling*. New York: John Wiley & Sons, Inc. 1967.

Siegel, Sidney. *Nonparametric Statistics for the Behavioral Sciences*. New York: McGraw-Hill, Inc. 1956.

Tuckman, Bruce W. *Conducting Educational Research*. New York: Harcourt Brace Javanovich, Inc., 1972.

Winer, B.J. *Statistical Principles in Experimental Design*. New York: McGraw-Hill, Inc., 1971.

INDEX

A

Achievement tests, 31
Activity: definition, 6; understanding, 5
Administration (see, Managing an evaluation)
Analysis of Covariance (ANCOVA): ANOVA as form of, 57; description, 57; design strategy, 58; evaluation questions and, 58; example, energy conservation program, 58; Information Collection Plan, 58; interpretation of analysis, 59
Analysis of evaluation information: ANCOVA, 57-59; ANOVA, 52-57; Chi square method, 63-66; conducting the analysis, 66; correlation statistics, 49-50; descriptive statistics, 48; evaluation proposal, inclusion, 89; Health Education Program, sample of results, 78-79; Information Analysis Plan (IAP), 69-70; interpretation of results, 67 (see also, Interpretation of analysis); methods, in general, 47; MANOVA, 59-63; Newman-Keuls method, 53, 55, 57; organization of, 43-46; pilot tests of activities, 66; planning activities, 4; regression, 50; report of, 73 (see also, Report of evaluation information); (see also, Interpretation of analysis)
Analysis of variance (ANOVA): ANCOVA as form of, 57; evaluation questions, 52; example of use, 54; F-statistics, 53; in general, 52; null hypothesis, 53
ANCOVA (see, Analysis of Covariance)
ANOVA (see, Analysis of Variance)
Archive reviews, 28
Assignment of evaluation staff, 4, 83

B

Budget: details, 84-88; evaluation proposal, inclusion, 90; management, 4

C

Campbell, Donald T., 13
Case evaluation design: example, 15; sampling procedures, 20-25 (see also, Design strategy)
Chi square: contingency tables, 64, 65; design strategy and, 65; evaluation questions and, 65; goodness-of-fit table, 64; use of, 63
Coding information, 43
Collection of information (see, Information collection)
Comparison group designs: description, 17; quasi-experimental group, example, 17; sampling procedures, 20; true experimental comparison group design, example, 19 (see also, Design strategy)
Concurrent validity, 40
Construct validity, 40
Content validity, 40
Contingency tables, 64, 65
Correlation statistics, 62
Costs for evaluation (see, Budget)
Covariant, definition, 57 (see also, Analysis of covariance)
Criterion-referenced tests, 33

D

Data (see, Analysis of evaluation information; Information collection)
Degrees of freedom, F-values for, 53
Dependent variables, 21; Evaluation Design Description, 22 (see also, Variables)
Descriptive statistics, 48; use with MANOVA, 61
Design strategy: case design, 15; comparison group designs, 17; construction, in general, 3, 13; effectiveness evaluation, 3; Evaluation Design Description, example, 21-23; evaluation proposals, inclusion, 89; evaluation report, description, 72; external validity, 14; Health Education Program, sample, 76; improvement evaluation, 3; information collection, limitations on, 35; internal validity, 13; time series designs, 16

E

Effectiveness evaluation: analysis methods, 4; design strategy, 3; external evaluator, role, 4; information collection, 3; questions, 3; purpose of, 2; reporting, 4 (see also, Improvement evaluation)